I0049126

Facebook

Marketing

How to Grow Your Business Using Facebook

(Highly Effective Strategies for Business Advertising Generating Sales and Passive Income)

Mark Salazar

Published By **Jenna Olsen**

Mark Salazar

All Rights Reserved

Facebook Marketing: How to Grow Your Business Using Facebook (Highly Effective Strategies for Business Advertising Generating Sales and Passive Income)

ISBN 978-1-7752967-8-2

No part of this guidebook shall be reproduced in any form without permission in writing from the publisher except in the case of brief quotations embodied in critical articles or reviews.

Legal & Disclaimer

The information contained in this book is not designed to replace or take the place of any form of medicine or professional medical advice. The information in this book has been provided for educational & entertainment purposes only.

The information contained in this book has been compiled from sources deemed reliable, and it is accurate to the best of the Author's knowledge; however, the Author cannot guarantee its accuracy and validity and cannot be held liable for any errors or omissions. Changes are periodically made to this book. You must consult your doctor or get professional medical advice before using any of the suggested remedies, techniques, or information in this book.

Table Of Contents

Chapter 1: Understanding The Face Book Landscape

In the huge expanse of the digital realm, Face e-book stands as a massive landscape, supplying both opportunities and demanding conditions for organizations attempting to find to thrive within the on-line space. To navigate this dynamic platform efficaciously, it's far essential to delve into the intricacies of the Face book panorama. In this monetary disaster, we are capable of embark on a journey to understand the foundational elements that shape the Face book revel in for users and entrepreneurs alike.

The Evolution of Face book:

Begin by using the usage of tracing the evolution of Face book, from its humble origins as a college networking platform to its modern-day-day reputation as a worldwide social media huge. Explore key milestones, acquisitions, and the factors which have contributed to its dominance inside the virtual panorama.

User Demographics and Behavior:

Uncover the diverse demographics that constitute the big individual base of Face book. Understand individual behavior patterns, options, and the tactics in which people interact with content. A nuanced comprehension of your target market lays the muse for crafting targeted and resonant advertising techniques.

Business Pages and Profiles:

Dive into the location of organization pages and profiles on Face book. Learn a manner to create an impactful industrial corporation page those not simplest showcases your brand however additionally serves as a hub for client interaction. Explore the abilties and gear available to organizations, from compelling visuals to informative content.

The Algorithmic Landscape:

Decipher the complicated workings of the Facebook set of guidelines. Understand how the platform determines the visibility of content material material in customers' feeds, considering elements including engagement, relevance, and timeliness. Stay abreast of algorithmic updates to conform your marketing and marketing techniques correctly.

Content Dynamics:

Content is the lifeblood of Facebook. Explore the severa varieties of content fabric fabric—from textual content posts and images to movies and interactive factors—that captivate and engage clients. Learn the art work of crafting content that resonates with your aim market and aligns with the ever-evolving alternatives of Facebook customers.

Community Building and Groups:

Beyond individual profiles and business corporation pages, Facebook fosters businesses via companies. Explore the dynamics of community building and find out how creating or participating in groups can beautify your brand's presence. Understand the position of engagement and interplay in cultivating a devoted network.

Privacy and Security Considerations:

As privateness concerns benefit prominence within the virtual landscape, delve into the privateness and safety abilties on Facebook. Understand the measures in vicinity to protect character facts and the way groups can navigate the evolving panorama of facts protection while retaining take transport of as genuine with with their target marketplace.

Advertising Opportunities:

Uncover the numerous advertising and advertising and advertising possibilities that Facebook gives. From backed posts and carousel advertisements to focused campaigns, find out the system to be had to growth your logo's obtain and connect with precise target audience segments.

Understand the nuances of Facebook Ads to maximize their impact.

By the surrender of this financial ruin, you could have acquired a entire understanding of the multifaceted Facebook panorama. Armed with this information, you'll be organized to traverse the terrain strategically, laying the inspiration for powerful Facebook advertising within the chapters that follow.

1.1 The Evolution of Facebook

In the annals of the internet's history, few systems have left as indelible a mark as Facebook. Born inside the hallowed halls of Harvard University in 2004, this social media behemoth has handed via a terrific evolution, reworking from a university-centric networking tool proper right into a international strain that permeates the cloth of our interconnected lives.

1.   Founding Vision:

The genesis of Facebook can be traced to the fertile mind of Mark Zuckerberg, along together with his college roommates Andrew McCollum, Eduardo Saverin, Chris Hughes, and Dustin Moskovitz. The platform, initially called "Facebook," changed into conceived as an internet listing for Harvard college university college students, supplying a virtual location for social connection in the university.

2.   Collegiate Conquest:

Facebook fast outgrew its Ivy League origins, spreading its wings to certainly one of a type universities and faculties at some stage in the USA and past. The appeal of connecting with friends, sharing evaluations, and growing one's social circle fueled Facebook's speedy increase, establishing it because the preeminent social networking platform for the collegiate demographic.

three. The Social Media Revolution:

As the 2000s spread out, Facebook spearheaded a broader societal shift inside the direction of social media as a number one mode of communique. Its intuitive interface, coupled with functions much like the News Feed and the introduction of the long-lasting "Like" button in 2009, propelled Facebook into mainstream recognition. The platform have grow to be a virtual city square, in which humans may want to percentage their thoughts, pics, and existence updates with a worldwide target marketplace.

four.   Open to All:

Sensing the functionality for a more expansive impact, Facebook made a pivotal preference in 2006: it opened its doorways to the overall public. No longer confined to the academic realm, Facebook have turn out to be accessible to everyone with a valid e mail deal with, marking a turning aspect in its journey in the direction of international ubiquity.

5.   Mobile Revolution:

Recognizing the developing tide of cell generation, Facebook underwent a transformative shift towards cell-centric tales.

The release of the Facebook app in 2010 ushered in a modern day generation, allowing customers to engage with the platform each time, everywhere. Mobile compatibility have become a cornerstone of Facebook's technique, aligning with the more and more mobile-centric way of existence of its clients.

6.   Acquisitions and Integrations:

Facebook's growth end up no longer completely natural; strategic acquisitions played a pivotal characteristic. The acquisition of Instagram in 2012 and WhatsApp in 2014 prolonged Facebook's portfolio, integrating famous structures that resonated with incredible patron bases. These acquisitions now not best reinforced Facebook's client numbers but additionally placed the agency as a multifaceted social media conglomerate.

7.   The Rise of Video:

With the appearance of excessive-velocity internet, video content won prominence. Facebook replied through prioritizing video skills, introducing autoplay movies, and Facebook Live in 2015. The platform converted right into a dynamic seen medium, accommodating the developing urge for food for video content material material material amongst clients and advertisers alike.

8.   Challenges and Controversies:

Facebook's meteoric upward thrust has not been without its share of annoying situations. The platform faced scrutiny over privateness issues, information breaches, and its characteristic inside the dissemination of incorrect records. Mark Zuckerberg's appearances in advance than congressional committees and a heightened attention on privateness settings underscored the platform's dedication to addressing those issues and fostering a more strong on-line environment.

9.   Beyond the News Feed:

As customer selections superior, Facebook tailored with the aid of using diversifying its content fabric transport mechanisms. The introduction of Stories in 2017 supplied a extra ephemeral and immersive manner for customers to percentage moments. Facebook Marketplace emerged as a platform for buying and promoting, further increasing Facebook's software program beyond social interaction.

10.   Augmented Reality and the Future:

Looking earlier, Facebook has set its sights at the frontier of augmented fact (AR). The development of technology like Facebook Horizon and the mixing of AR competencies into the platform symptoms a determination to shaping the subsequent wave of virtual interaction, wherein the bounds a number of the physical and virtual worlds blur.

Chapter 2: Setting The Foundation

In the dynamic realm of Facebook advertising and advertising and advertising, success hinges on a strong basis. This financial spoil lays the foundation on your journey, offering insights into the critical factors that form the bedrock of an powerful Facebook marketing approach. From putting in place a compelling industrial organisation profile to information your target market, every side is a critical building block essential for a sturdy and sustainable presence on this social media large.

Crafting an Irresistible Business Page:

Your enterprise net web page is the digital storefront of your logo on Facebook. Explore the artwork of crafting an not possible to stand up to commercial organization web web page that not only captivates site visitors however moreover communicates your logo identification correctly. From deciding on compelling visuals to writing attractive content material cloth, every element plays a function in shaping the number one impact traffic have of your business employer.

Optimizing Profile and Cover Images:

Dive into the nuances of profile and cowl images. Understand the dimensions, choice, and layout ideas that make those visuals stand out. Your profile and cover photos are the seen ambassadors of your emblem, and optimizing them guarantees that your corporation is supplied inside the first rate mild.

Compelling About Section:

The 'About' phase is your possibility to inform your logo's tale. Explore the factors that make a compelling 'About' phase, from concise but informative descriptions to strategically located key terms. This section serves as a concise creation to your industrial agency, conveying crucial information and welcoming clients to look at more.

Contact Information and Business Details:

Ensure that your contact information and organisation statistics are certainly reachable. Explore the importance of accurate and up to date records, along with your deal with, cellular telephone amount, and net site. Easy accessibility complements man or woman experience and fosters agree with with functionality customers.

Understanding Facebook Insights:

Facebook offers a treasure trove of facts through Insights. Delve into the arena of analytics and apprehend a manner to interpret key metrics. From gain and engagement to demographic insights, Facebook Insights empowers you to evaluate the general overall performance of your content material fabric and refine your technique for max impact.

Defining Your Target Audience:

One period does no longer healthy all in the realm of Facebook advertising and marketing and advertising. Understand the significance of defining your goal marketplace with precision. Explore tools and techniques for figuring out and accomplishing the goal marketplace that is maximum likely to engage together together along with your content material and convert it into customers.

Setting SMART Goals:

Goals offer route on your Facebook advertising efforts. Learn the way to set SMART dreams—Specific, Measurable, Achievable, Relevant, and Time-positive. Whether it's far developing logo reputation, riding internet website on-line traffic, or boosting sales, a clean purpose-setting framework courses your method and measures success.

Content Strategy Essentials:

Content is the overseas coins of engagement on Facebook. Explore the necessities of a sturdy content material fabric method, from records the high-quality posting frequency to diversifying content codecs. Whether it is informative articles, fascinating visuals, or interactive polls, a nicely-rounded content approach keeps your aim marketplace engaged and coming once more for added.

Building a Content Calendar:

Consistency is excessive in Facebook advertising and advertising and marketing. Dive into the paintings of building a content fabric fabric calendar that aligns together with your desires and resonates together together with your target marketplace. A nicely-prepared content material cloth calendar ensures a consistent flow of appealing content material fabric and lets in you live in advance of dispositions and activities relevant to your target market.

Engagement Strategies:

Engagement is the coronary heart beat of Facebook marketing. Explore strategies to foster huge interactions together collectively together with your purpose marketplace, from responding at once to remarks to starting up discussions. Building a community spherical your emblem involves active engagement, remodeling passive observers into dedicated fans and advocates.

As we delve into the intricacies of placing the inspiration, recall that each element is interconnected, contributing to the overarching fulfillment of your Facebook advertising and marketing method. By studying the ones foundational ideas, you aren't simply developing a presence on Facebook; you are constructing a dynamic and sustainable platform for your emblem to thrive within the virtual landscape.

2.1 Creating a Business Page

In the expansive worldwide of social media, a Facebook Business Page serves as a pivotal hub for connecting together at the side of your goal market, constructing logo identification, and the usage of engagement. This step-by using way of way of-step manual will walk you thru the technique of making a compelling and expert Facebook Business

Page that captures the essence of your emblem.

Log into Your Personal Facebook Account:

Begin through logging into your private Facebook account. If you do not have one, you may need to create it. Once logged in, navigate to the menu on the pinnacle proper corner of the show screen, click on on on the downward arrow, and choose "Create Page."

Choose a Page Category:

Facebook offers one-of-a-kind training for enterprise pages, which consist of "Business or Brand," "Community or Public Figure," and greater. Select the category that best aligns collectively in conjunction with your employer or brand. Then, pick out a extra unique magnificence from the dropdown menu and enter your employer call.

Complete Basic Information:

Fill out the simple statistics to your enterprise, together with your enterprise address, cell telephone amount, and internet site. Providing correct and updated data is crucial for customers seeking out to connect with your commercial enterprise.

Add a Profile Picture:

Choose a profile photo that represents your logo visually. This may be your logo or every other image that people companion collectively along with your commercial company. Ensure the photograph is apparent, amazing, and recognizable even in smaller dimensions.

Create a Striking Cover Photo:

Your cover picture is a high visible actual belongings in your agency page. Design an eye catching cowl picture that presentations your logo's character. This can be a product display off, a at the back of-the-scenes photo, or some thing that encapsulates the essence of your company.

Customize Your Page:

Navigate to the "Edit Page Info" section to offer more information approximately your commercial organization. This consists of an extensive description, agency hours, project, and greater. The extra data you offer, the less complex it's miles for site visitors to recognize what your industrial agency is all about.

Create a Username (Vanity URL):

Customize your internet web page's URL to make it effortlessly shareable and excellent. This is likewise called a "arrogance URL" and typically appears as facebook.Com/yourbusinessname. A concise and relevant username enhances your web page's accessibility.

Add a Call-to-Action Button:

Direct net website online site visitors to take particular movements on your web page by means of the use of using inclusive of a call-to-motion (CTA) button. Whether it is "Shop Now," "Contact Us," or "Learn More," choose a CTA that aligns together with your commercial enterprise organisation dreams and encourages person interaction.

Populate Your Page with Content:

Before inviting people to love your internet web page, populate it with initial content fabric. Create attractive posts, percentage relevant articles, and display off your services or products. An lively and colourful web page is more likely to attract and keep fans.

Invite Your Network:

Once your web internet web page is installation and populated with content cloth, invite your friends, colleagues, and present contacts to love and follow your net web page. This initial enhance enables kickstart your internet page's engagement and visibility.

Chapter 3: Crafting Compelling Content

In the ever-evolving landscape of Facebook advertising and marketing and advertising, content material cloth reigns high-quality. This financial ruin delves into the art and era of crafting compelling content material that captures interest, resonates together along with your target audience, and drives massive engagement. From knowledge the nuances of severa content material formats to studying the psychology of effective storytelling, this financial smash is your guide to growing content that now not simplest stops the scroll however leaves an prolonged-lasting effect.

Understanding Your Audience:

Demographic Insights: Delve into the demographics of your target audience the use of Facebook Insights. Understand their age, place, pastimes, and online conduct. This knowledge paperwork the inspiration for tailoring content cloth that speaks immediately to their options.

Diversifying Content Formats:

Visual Appeal: Leverage the strength of visuals with hobby-grabbing pix and films. Experiment with carousel posts, slideshows, and dynamic presentations to maintain your content visually stimulating.

Interactive Content: Engage your purpose market with interactive content material fabric which consist of polls, quizzes, and contests. Interactive factors foster participation, developing the opportunity of shares and feedback.

The Art of Storytelling:

Emotional Resonance: Craft narratives that evoke emotions. Whether it's far pleasure, empathy, or hobby, emotionally resonant memories create a connection with your purpose market.

Brand Narrative: Develop a cohesive emblem narrative that unfolds thru your content material cloth cloth. Consistency in storytelling strengthens emblem identification and fosters a enjoy of familiarity.

Strategic Use of Captions:

Concise and Impactful: Craft captions that are concise but impactful. Use compelling language to carry your message efficiently and inspire in addition engagement.

Intrigue and Curiosity: Spark hobby with captions that set off customers to analyze greater. Pose questions, percentage exciting records, or tease upcoming content cloth material to hold your target audience intrigued.

Timeliness and Relevance:

Stay Current: Keep your content material fabric properly timed via aligning it with modern events, vacations, and company inclinations. Timely content material will increase visibility and demonstrates your brand's attention of the arena round it.

Evergreen Content: Balance well timed content material cloth with evergreen pieces that stay relevant through the years. This ensures a consistent float of engaging content fabric cloth even in the course of quieter periods.

Content Calendar Planning:

Consistency: Develop a content material fabric calendar to hold a steady posting time table. Consistency fosters target market expectancies and guarantees that your emblem remains in your intention market's radar.

Variety: Plan for content cloth material variety to save you monotony. Mix promotional content material with informative posts, at the back of-the-scenes glimpses, and individual-generated content material material cloth to keep your feed numerous and interesting.

Quality Over Quantity:

High-Quality Visuals: Prioritize awesome visuals that align collectively together with your brand aesthetics. Crisp pictures, nicely-edited films, and expert pix decorate the perceived fee of your content material fabric.

Value-Driven Content: Ensure that every piece of content cloth fabric gives price in your target market. Whether it is amusement, information, or belief, content cloth must fulfill a motive for the viewer.

Optimizing for Facebook Algorithms:

Engagement Metrics: Understand Facebook's algorithmic factors, which incorporates character engagement, relevance, and timeliness. Craft content material material that encourages likes, feedback, and shares to decorate its visibility on clients' feeds.

Native Content: Utilize neighborhood talents which embody Facebook Live and local movies. Facebook has a tendency to prioritize content material material created internal its platform, principal to accelerated natural attain.

User-Generated Content (UGC):

Authenticity: Encourage your goal market to contribute for your content fabric thru UGC. User-generated content cloth fabric not most effective offers authenticity however moreover builds a feel of network spherical your emblem.

Showcasing Customers: Feature client testimonials, opinions, and memories. This now not only highlights your happy client base but additionally serves as social proof for ability customers.

Measuring and Adapting:

Analytics Evaluation: Regularly have a look at your content material everyday performance thru Facebook Insights. Identify immoderate-appearing content material and apprehend the opportunities of your target market.

Adaptation Strategies: Based on analytics, adapt your content approach. Focus on content material material formats and subjects that resonate most along with your target audience, optimizing for max impact.

As you embark on the adventure of crafting compelling content fabric to your Facebook Business Page, hold in thoughts that flexibility and versatility are key. Stay attuned to the feedback and options of your audience, allowing their insights to form your evolving content material material approach. In the subsequent chapters, we're going to discover superior methods and techniques to expand the effect of your content material cloth material at the dynamic platform that is Facebook.

3.1 Content Strategy for Facebook

In the bustling panorama of Facebook advertising, a well-described content approach is the compass that publications your logo through the digital terrain. This manual unravels the layers of creating an effective content material fabric approach tailored for Facebook, from understanding your target market to optimizing content cloth for algorithms and fostering community engagement.

1. Audience Research and Persona Development:

Demographic Insights: Utilize Facebook Insights to advantage valuable demographic information approximately your audience. Understand their age, place, pursuits, and on line behaviors to tell content cloth fabric advent.

Persona Development: Construct specific client personas based on your goal marketplace studies. These personas serve as archetypes representing the developments and possibilities of your purpose marketplace.

2. Content Objectives and Key Performance Indicators (KPIs):

Define Objectives: Clearly outline your content material material fabric goals.

Whether it is growing logo interest, the usage of net website web site traffic, or boosting engagement, articulate particular and measurable dreams.

Identify KPIs: Align key regular overall performance signs in conjunction with your objectives. Track metrics which includes achieve, engagement, click on-through expenses, and conversions to diploma the success of your content method.

3.   Content Mix and Diversity:

Varied Formats: Diversify your content fabric blend with numerous codecs. Incorporate images, motion pix, carousel posts, and interactive content cloth like polls and quizzes to keep your feed dynamic.

Educational and Entertaining Content: Balance promotional content material with academic and wonderful portions. Informative content positions your logo as an organisation authority, while exciting content fosters a connection with your aim market.

four.   Storytelling and Brand Narrative:

Consistent Brand Voice: Develop a normal brand voice in the course of your content cloth cloth. Whether it is witty and humorous or informative and expert, preserving a cohesive emblem narrative strengthens logo identity.

Story Arcs: Craft storytelling arcs that spread regularly. Take your target market on a journey, whether or not it's miles the evolution of your emblem, within the lower back of-the-scenes glimpses, or achievement stories.

5.   Content Calendar and Scheduling:

Regular Posting Schedule: Establish a steady posting time desk. A content material calendar guarantees that your audience gets a consistent go with the go with the flow of content material material, keeping their engagement and interest.

Event and Seasonal Planning: Plan content cloth round sports, holidays, and seasons.

Timely and relevant content enhances visibility and faucets into trending conversations.

6.   Engagement Strategies:

Community Building: Foster network engagement with the aid of actively responding to feedback and messages. Create content cloth material that sparks discussions and invitations participation, transforming your target market into an energetic community.

Contests and Challenges: Launch contests, traumatic situations, or giveaways to incentivize engagement. Encourage consumer-generated content material fabric and show off submissions to growth attain.

7.   Paid Advertising Integration:

Strategic Boosting: Integrate paid advertising and marketing strategically into your content material material method. Boost excessive-appearing posts to growth their acquire and leverage Facebook Ads to goal specific demographics aligned together collectively along with your company dreams.

A/B Testing: Experiment with A/B locating out to refine your paid advertising approach. Test exquisite ad creatives, purpose market segments, and ad placements to optimize regular overall performance.

8.   Data Analysis and Iteration:

Regular Analytics Review: Analyze content material ordinary ordinary overall performance the usage of Facebook Insights regularly. Identify top-acting content fabric and recognize target market interactions.

Iterative Strategy: Based on analytics, iterate your content material cloth method. Adjust posting times, content material material formats, and topics to align with target market alternatives, maximizing engagement and effect.

9.   Collaboration and Cross-Promotion:

Collaborative Content: Collaborate with influencers, companions, or distinctive organizations for collaborative content cloth. Cross-merchandising introduces your emblem to new audiences and enhances credibility through association.

Tagging and Mentions: Utilize tagging and mentions to hook up with special companies or humans to your content material. This not best broadens your obtain however furthermore nurtures relationships in the on-line community.

10.   Trends and Algorithm Adaptation:

Stay Current with Trends: Keep a watch on growing trends inside your industry and on Facebook. Incorporate trending subjects and formats to stay relevant and seize the eye of your audience.

Adapt to Algorithm Changes: Facebook's set of rules evolves. Stay informed approximately updates and adapt your content fabric technique for this reason. Understanding algorithmic elements guarantees that your content material cloth is optimized for visibility.

By weaving the ones factors into your content material cloth approach, you lay the inspiration for a dynamic and impactful presence on Facebook. Remember, a a success content fabric method isn't always static; it's miles a dwelling, evolving entity that responds to target market dynamics and the ever-changing digital panorama. In the following chapters, we are going to discover superior processes and strategies to elevate your Facebook content material material cloth endeavor.

three.2 Types of Content That Engage

Diversifying your content fabric is high to taking images and keeping the attention of your Facebook target audience. Here's a breakdown of numerous content cloth types that have examined to be attractive at the platform:

Visual Content:

High-Quality Images: Share visually appealing snap shots that exhibit your merchandise, offerings, or emblem individual. High-amazing visuals capture interest in the crowded Facebook feed.

Infographics: Condense complicated information into visually appealing infographics. These aren't handiest visually attractive however additionally powerful in conveying information speedy.

Video Content:

Short-form Videos: Create quick and snappy movement photos that rapid supply your message. With the upward push of brief-form content material fabric, platforms like Facebook opt for motion pix that capture interest inside the first few seconds.

Live Videos: Leverage Facebook Live to connect with your aim market in real time. Live movement pics inspire immediate interplay and engagement, as visitors can statement and react within the moment.

Interactive Content:

Polls and Surveys: Encourage target audience participation thru polls and surveys. People enjoy sharing their evaluations, and interactive content material cloth boosts engagement.

Quizzes: Create unique quizzes associated with your industry or emblem. Quizzes no longer quality entertain however moreover encourage customers to percent their outcomes, growing your acquire.

Chapter 4: Building A Community

In the region of Facebook marketing, the actual strength lies now not definitely in broadcasting your brand message but in fostering a colorful community around it. This financial disaster explores the strategies and standards within the again of constructing a sturdy and engaged community on Facebook, reworking passive enthusiasts into lively contributors and advocates.

1.   Understanding Community Dynamics:

Identifying Shared Interests: Recognize the shared hobbies and values that join your target market. Understanding what brings them together paperwork the premise for community constructing.

Two-Way Communication: Emphasize the importance of -manner communication. A community flourishes on communicate, where every the brand and its goal marketplace actively make contributions to conversations.

2.   Establishing Brand Personality:

Consistent Brand Voice: Develop and preserve a regular logo voice. A recognizable and actual personality makes your brand greater relatable, fostering a experience of familiarity in the community.

Humanizing Your Brand: Showcase the human facet of your logo. Share at the back of-the-scenes glimpses, introduce group individuals, and take part in discussions as real people rather than organisation entities.

3.   Content that Fosters Interaction:

Provocative Questions: Pose questions that provoke thoughtful responses. Encourage your community people to percentage their evaluations, memories, and insights.

Interactive Challenges: Launch interactive challenges that invite network participation. Challenges, contests, or themed sports create a feel of camaraderie and pleasure.

four.   Active Community Management:

Timely Responses: Prioritize nicely timed responses to comments, messages, and network posts. Active control indicates that your logo values and appreciates the contributions of its network.

Moderation Guidelines: Establish smooth moderation guidelines. A well-moderated community ensures a brilliant and respectful environment for all contributors.

five.   Exclusive Content and Offers:

Member-Only Content: Provide one in all a type content material or early get entry to to network human beings. Exclusive perks make individuals experience valued and encourage others to join the community.

Special Offers: Offer special promotions or discounts entirely for community members. This now not only drives engagement however moreover rewards your maximum dependable fans.

6.   Community Events and Initiatives:

Virtual Events: Host digital sports activities inside the community. Live Q&A durations, webinars, or virtual meetups enhance the texture of community and provide valuable interactions.

Community Challenges: Create demanding conditions or tasks that rally the community round a commonplace aim. This may additionally need to encompass collaborative obligations, charity drives, or shared milestones.

7. Encouraging User-Generated Content (UGC):

UGC Contests: Run contests that encourage individuals to create and percentage content. UGC no longer best sparks creativity however furthermore showcases the range and enthusiasm of your network.

Highlighting UGC: Regularly characteristic UGC to your web page. This acknowledgment no longer most effective rewards individuals however moreover inspires others to actively participate.

8.   Community Guidelines and Values:

Clear Guidelines: Establish easy community recommendations. Clearly speak expectancies regarding respectful conversation, content material fabric sharing, and ultra-modern community conduct.

Values Alignment: Ensure that the community aligns collectively with your logo values. A shared set of values fosters a cohesive and supportive environment.

nine.   Recognizing and Celebrating Members:

Member Spotlights: Regularly highlight community members. Highlighting man or woman contributions strengthens the feel of belonging and encourages endured engagement.

Community Milestones: Celebrate network milestones and achievements. Whether it's far accomplishing a positive member rely or finishing a community undertaking, milestones foster a experience of shared accomplishment.

10.   Feedback and Collaboration:

Seeking Feedback: Actively are attempting to find for remarks from the network. Whether it's far about products, content fabric, or community tasks, associated with participants in preference-making complements their enjoy of ownership.

Collaborative Decision-Making: Involve the community in collaborative selection-making techniques. This should encompass voting on new capabilities, deciding on topics for sports activities, or contributing thoughts for destiny initiatives.

Building a thriving community on Facebook is an ongoing adventure that calls for self-control, proper engagement, and a dedication to fostering connections. As you navigate the course of network building, keep in mind that the power of your community lies not just in its length but in the intensity of the relationships and shared studies amongst its people. In the approaching chapters, we are going to discover advanced techniques to raise your community engagement on Facebook.

4.1 Growing Your Facebook Audience

The success of your Facebook presence hinges on the energy and duration of your target market. This financial disaster unveils techniques and techniques to strategically extend and have interaction your Facebook purpose market. From natural boom strategies to leveraging advertising, this guide equips you with the gadget to maximize your attain and cultivate a severa and engaged network.

1.   Optimize Your Profile for Discovery:

Complete Profile Information: Ensure your Facebook Business Page is complete with accurate and compelling information. A well-optimized profile will increase the danger of appearing in relevant searches.

Utilize Keywords: Infuse relevant key phrases for your profile and posts. This complements the discoverability of your content at the same time as clients look for subjects related to your place of interest.

2.   Create Shareable and Viral Content:

Compelling Visuals: Craft visually attractive content that stands proud within the information feed. Shareable visuals have the capability to transport viral, increasing your reap exponentially.

Emotionally Resonant Content: Create content cloth that evokes feelings. Emotional resonance encourages clients to percent content material with their network, introducing your emblem to new audiences.

3.   Engage with Existing Communities:

Join Relevant Groups: Participate in Facebook businesses related to your industry or vicinity of hobby. Engage in discussions, offer precious insights, and subtly promote your web page at the same time as applicable.

Collaborate in Communities: Collaborate with unique agencies or influencers inside your community. This skip-promoting can introduce your net web page to new audiences.

4.   Regular Posting and Consistency:

Frequent Posting: Post usually to maintain visibility for your enthusiasts' data feeds. Regular posting fosters a enjoy of continuity and encourages ongoing engagement.

Optimal Posting Times: Identify exceptional posting instances primarily based totally on even as your purpose market is most lively. This ensures that your content material reaches the most extensive type of clients.

5.   Leverage Facebook Ads:

Targeted Advertising: Utilize centered Facebook Ads to attain unique demographics aligned collectively along side your employer desires. The platform's robust focused on options will allow you to tailor your advertisements to benefit the most relevant goal marketplace.

Promote Engaging Content: Boost immoderate-acting herbal content material fabric with paid promotions. This extends the reach of successful posts to a much wider intention market.

6.   Host Contests and Giveaways:

Encourage Participation: Host contests or giveaways that require participants to love, percentage, or tag friends. This not only boosts engagement however also expands your page's visibility.

Collaborative Giveaways: Collaborate with particular groups for joint giveaways. This introduces your net internet web page to the accomplice's target marketplace, facilitating mutual boom.

7.   Implement Facebook Live Sessions:

Interactive Live Q&A: Conduct live Q&A periods or interactive discussions. Live movies usually tend to get maintain of better visibility in information feeds, and actual-time engagement can considerably increase your audience.

Teasers and Behind-the-Scenes: Offer extremely good within the returned of-the-scenes glimpses or product teasers inside the direction of stay commands. This specific content material fabric encourages clients to tune in often.

eight. Utilize Cross-Promotion Tactics:

Cross-Promote on Other Platforms: Promote your Facebook net page on extraordinary social media structures, your internet internet site on line, and in e mail newsletters. Cross-merchandising directs contemporary audiences for your Facebook internet web page.

Encourage Cross-Platform Sharing: Create content material fabric that encourages bypass-platform sharing. For instance, percentage snippets of Facebook-exquisite content on wonderful structures, prompting clients to go to your internet page for the complete revel in.

9.   Collaborate with Influencers:

Identify Relevant Influencers: Collaborate with influencers relevant on your corporation. Influencers deliver their hooked up target audience, providing an road for your emblem to be brought to a cutting-edge and engaged following.

Co-Create Content: Work with influencers to co-create content material material. This collaboration not handiest leverages their have an effect on but moreover gives range for your content material cloth.

10.   Engage with Trends and Hashtags:

Stay Trend-Aware: Keep an eye fixed on trending topics and hashtags. Incorporate relevant tendencies into your content material fabric to align with modern-day conversations and boom discoverability.

Create Branded Hashtags: Introduce branded hashtags to your campaigns or network. Encourage customers to apply those hashtags in their posts, developing a cohesive and discoverable series of content material cloth.

As you enforce those strategies, consider that concentrate on target audience boom is a gradual technique that requires consistency and versatility. Monitor analytics, refine your method based totally totally mostly on what resonates collectively along with your target market, and remain open to evolving inclinations and techniques. In the following chapters, we're going to delve deeper into superior strategies for target marketplace engagement and brand amplification on Facebook.

5.2 Fostering Engagement and Interaction

Engagement is the lifeblood of a thriving Facebook presence. This financial disaster explores superior strategies to foster substantial interactions, create a enjoy of community, and hold your goal market actively engaged at the aspect of your content. From interactive features to community-building responsibilities, these procedures are designed to transform casual fans into unswerving advocates.

1.   Utilize Interactive Features:

Polls and Surveys: Leverage Facebook's ballot feature to build up evaluations from your target marketplace. Ask questions associated with your employer, upcoming merchandise, or their alternatives. This now not best sparks engagement however additionally gives precious insights.

Chapter 5: Advanced Advertising Techniques

Advertising on Facebook has developed into a complex and effective tool for groups to benefit their audience. This financial smash explores advanced techniques and strategies to raise your advertising and advertising and marketing efforts at the platform. From precision centered on to revolutionary optimization, those techniques are designed to maximise the effectiveness of your Facebook advertisements.

1.   Advanced Targeting Strategies:

Custom Audiences: Utilize custom audiences based totally on person interactions together with your internet page, net web website online, or unique content material cloth. Tailor your classified ads to taken into consideration one in every of a type segments of your target audience, ensuring custom designed and relevant messaging.

Lookalike Audiences: Leverage lookalike audiences to make bigger your obtain.

Facebook identifies customers with traits much like your present audience, improving the hazard of accomplishing capability customers.

2. Dynamic Ads for Personalized Campaigns:

Dynamic Product Ads: Implement dynamic product commercials to showcase customized content material material based on the person's surfing facts or previous interactions collectively at the side of your net website on line. This quite personalized technique will growth the relevance of your commercials.

Dynamic Ad Creative: Use dynamic ad progressive that robotically populates with applicable data, which incorporates product names or prices. This streamlines the advertising and advertising and marketing and advertising and marketing and advertising technique and guarantees real-time accuracy.

three. A/B Testing for Optimization:

Creative Elements: Conduct A/B sorting out on incredible contemporary factors, together with snap shots, headlines, and ad duplicate. Analyze typical performance metrics to choose out out the high-quality mixtures on your target market.

Ad Placements: Test severa ad placements, such as in-feed, stories, or the right column. Assess in which your advertisements carry out notable to allocate the price range strategically.

4.   Retargeting Strategies:

Pixel-Based Retargeting: Implement pixel-primarily based completely absolutely retargeting to attain customers who have visited your net internet web page however have now not finished the popular actions, which incorporates creating a buy. Remind them of products or services they viewed.

Sequential Messaging: Create sequential ad campaigns that tell a story or guide customers through a funnel. Tailor messaging primarily based at the individual's preceding interactions collectively along with your emblem.

5.   Video Advertising Optimization:

Captivating Thumbnails: Optimize video advert thumbnails to be visually compelling. A putting thumbnail encourages customers to prevent scrolling and have interaction along with your video content material.

Engagement Metrics: Track engagement metrics for video commercials, in conjunction with watch time, click on on-through expenses, and finishing touch costs. Use this records to refine your video content material method.

6.   Conversion Rate Optimization (CRO):

Landing Page Testing: Conduct A/B attempting out on landing pages to optimize for conversions. Test extraordinary layouts, messaging, and calls to movement to come to be privy to the tremendous mixtures.

Mobile Optimization: Ensure that your landing pages are optimized for mobile customers. Mobile-friendly research make contributions to better conversion charges.

7.   Ad Scheduling for Peak Performance:

Time-of-Day Targeting: Utilize advert scheduling to aim specific times of the day or week on the equal time as your goal market is most active. This ensures that your commercials appear inside the route of pinnacle engagement periods.

Dayparting Strategies: Experiment with dayparting techniques to regulate bids or budgets sooner or later of particular hours. Allocate property based on at the same time as your target market is much more likely to convert.

eight. Ad Creative Innovation: Interactive Ads: Explore interactive advert codecs that inspire purchaser engagement, along with playable commercials or augmented reality research. Interactive factors enhance character participation and memorability.

Carousel Ads for Storytelling: Use carousel commercials to tell a visible tale. Each card inside the carousel can carry a unique element of your message, retaining clients engaged and curious.

nine. Advanced Bid Strategies:

Cost Cap Bidding: Implement charge cap bidding to govern the fee of handing over your ads even as maximizing outcomes. This technique permits you to set a most cost steady with stop give up result.

Bid Adjustments: Utilize bid adjustments based on elements on the aspect of tool type, place, or audience demographics. Adjusting bids for specific necessities can optimize your advert shipping.

10. Attribution Modeling for Insights:

Multi-Touch Attribution: Explore multi-touch attribution models to recognize the complete consumer journey. This gives insights into the severa touchpoints that make a contribution to conversions.

Custom Attribution Models: Create custom attribution fashions tailor-made to your business corporation goals. Develop models that prioritize particular touchpoints or interactions to align together together with your specific conversion direction.

As you venture into advanced advertising and marketing on Facebook, take into account to usually have a have a look at ordinary overall performance metrics and adapt your techniques primarily based definitely on the evolving landscape. The combination of specific centered on, innovative innovation, and records-pushed optimization positions your Facebook commercials for max effect. In the imminent chapters, we are capable of delve into techniques for measuring ROI and leveraging analytics to refine your advertising and marketing and advertising and marketing efforts further.

5.1 Facebook Ads Essentials

Unlocking the general functionality of Facebook advertising and advertising and advertising calls for a sturdy know-how of the requirements. This bankruptcy serves as a whole guide to the essential factors that shape the spine of a fulfillment Facebook advert campaigns. From marketing campaign objectives to advert formats and target audience concentrated on, this roadmap will equip you with the records to craft powerful and impactful Facebook advertisements.

1.   Defining Clear Campaign Objectives:

Awareness, Consideration, Conversion: Align your ad marketing and advertising and marketing marketing marketing campaign with specific desires. Choose amongst awareness, attention, or conversion desires to tailor your technique and measure success efficiently.

Campaign Goals Alignment: Ensure that your marketing campaign objectives align together

together with your broader marketing and advertising and advertising and business enterprise dreams. This readability courses your advert technique in the direction of tangible results.

2.   Audience Targeting Strategies:

Custom Audiences: Leverage custom audiences to cause clients based mostly on interactions together with your internet site, app, or preceding ad engagement. This allows for precise centered on of cutting-edge clients or warm temperature leads.

Lookalike Audiences: Extend your attain with lookalike audiences, centered on clients with tendencies just like your current consumer base. This technique taps into Facebook's algorithm to discover potential clients.

3.   Ad Creative Best Practices:

Compelling Visuals: Craft visually appealing and applicable pix or movies. Visuals are the primary detail of touch along side your purpose market and play a crucial function in capturing attention.

Clear and Concise Copy: Write easy, concise, and compelling advert reproduction. Clearly talk your message and price proposition, appealing customers to do so.

4.   Ad Formats and Placement Strategies:

In-Feed Ads: Utilize in-feed advertisements for seamless integration into users' information feeds. These advertisements appear as neighborhood content material, improving man or woman experience.

Stories Ads: Leverage Stories advertisements for a visually immersive enjoy. Capitalize on the general-display layout to engage customers with charming visuals and concise messaging.

5.   Budgeting and Bidding Strategies:

Daily and Lifetime Budgets: Choose among each day and lifelong budgets based totally totally in your advertising advertising and marketing marketing campaign goals. Daily budgets allocate price variety on a each day basis, at the equal time as lifetime budgets permit more flexibility over the advertising campaign duration.

Bidding Strategies: Experiment with bidding strategies, along with fee constant with click on (CPC) or fee in keeping with thousand impressions (CPM), to optimize for your marketing campaign dreams. Choose the bidding technique that aligns together with your objectives.

6. Ad Scheduling and Delivery Optimization:

Ad Scheduling: Use ad scheduling to manipulate even as your classified ads are proven. This function lets in you to purpose unique days and times whilst your goal marketplace is maximum active.

Delivery Optimization: Optimize ad shipping for specific actions, collectively with hyperlink clicks or conversions. This ensures that your budget is allocated closer to the consequences maximum vital to your advertising and advertising marketing campaign.

7.   Monitoring and Analytics:

Facebook Pixel Integration: Install the Facebook Pixel to your internet website on-line to tune consumer interactions. The pixel offers valuable facts for measuring conversions, optimizing advertisements, and developing centered audiences.

Conversion Tracking: Implement conversion tracking to degree the success of your ad campaigns. Track moves collectively with purchases, sign-ups, or form submissions to assess the impact of your classified ads.

eight. Ad Testing and Iteration:

A/B Testing: Conduct A/B trying out to evaluate particular ad elements and strategies. Test variables inclusive of headlines, visuals, and audience segments to choose out high-performing combos.

Iterative Optimization: Continuously study overall performance metrics and iterate your advertisements based totally on insights. This iterative technique guarantees ongoing improvement and flexibility to converting goal marketplace dynamics.

nine.   Ad Compliance and Guidelines:

Ad Policy Adherence: Familiarize your self with Facebook's ad guidelines and recommendations. Ensure that your advertisements follow the ones pointers to save you disapproval or restrict.

Ad Content Restrictions: Be aware of content material policies related to touchy subjects, language, and imagery. Adhering to those suggestions keeps a powerful person experience.

10.   Mobile Optimization:

Responsive Design: Optimize your ad innovative and landing pages for cell customers. With a big a part of Facebook customers getting access to the platform via cellular gadgets, responsive layout is vital for effective ad transport.

Fast Loading Times: Ensure that your advert content material cloth material and touchdown pages load speedy on mobile devices. Slow-loading pages can purpose man or woman frustration and accelerated soar costs.

By learning those Facebook Ads requirements, you installation a sturdy basis for a achievement campaigns. Regularly examine and update your techniques in response to analytics, purpose market comments, and evolving platform talents. In the following chapters, we'll explore advanced strategies to raise your Facebook advertising sport similarly.

6.2 Targeting and Custom Audiences

In the tough worldwide of Facebook advertising and marketing, precision concentrated on is the vital factor to unlocking campaigns that resonate collectively together with your target market. This financial ruin delves into advanced techniques for honing your concentrated on abilities and leveraging custom audiences to maximise the impact of your commercials.

1.   Advanced Demographic Targeting:

Demographic Segmentation: Refine your centered on through way of demographics which incorporates age, gender, area, and language. Drill down into particular segments to tailor your message to the traits of your perfect target market.

Life Events: Leverage existence event concentrated on to reap clients experiencing high-quality milestones, which include weddings, graduations, or shifting to a cutting-edge-day metropolis. Align your products or services with these existence sports for heightened relevance.

2.   Behavioral Targeting Tactics:

User Behavior Insights: Utilize Facebook's wealth of character behavior information.

Target users primarily based on their on line behavior, collectively with internet website online visits, app utilization, and interactions with Facebook content material.

Purchase Behavior: Fine-song your targeted on with the aid of considering users' purchase conduct. Target humans who've tested a bent toward comparable products or services.

3.   Interests and Hobbies Targeting:

Interest-Based Targeting: Leverage pursuits and pastimes focused on to align your advertisements with customers' passions. Identify applicable pursuits related to your area of interest to ensure your advertisements resonate with engaged and enthusiastic audiences.

Pages Liked and Followed: Target users primarily based on the Facebook Pages they prefer or take a look at. This approach faucets into customers' affinities, connecting your emblem with folks who already specific interest in related content material material.

4.   Custom Audiences Strategies:

Website Custom Audiences (WCA): Harness the strength of Website Custom Audiences to goal customers who have interacted together with your net website. Create segments based totally on unique pages visited, time spent on internet site on-line, or movements taken.

Engagement Custom Audiences: Build audiences from customer interactions at the facet of your Facebook content material fabric. Target the ones who've engaged together with your net web web page, advertisements, or sports activities to capitalize on current emblem affinity.

Customer List Uploads: Upload client lists to create custom audiences. Utilize e-mail addresses or telephone numbers to re-engage present clients or nurture leads thru centered advertisements.

Chapter 6: Measuring Success

In the dynamic landscape of Facebook advertising, fulfillment is not just about visibility; it's far about understanding the impact of your efforts. This financial catastrophe delves into the vital metrics, gear, and strategies for measuring success on the platform, imparting you with the insights needed to refine your method and accumulate meaningful results.

1.   Key Performance Indicators (KPIs):

Define Clear KPIs: Establish specific Key Performance Indicators aligned along side your advertising and advertising campaign goals. Whether it's brand interest, engagement, conversions, or a aggregate, readability on KPIs guides your size technique.

2.   Reach and Impressions:

Reach vs. Impressions: Differentiate amongst gain and impressions. Reach measures the specific customers who see your content material cloth material, even as impressions account for the whole form of instances your content material material is displayed. Monitoring each metrics gives a entire view of your content material material fabric's effect.

three. Engagement Metrics:

Likes, Comments, Shares: Track engagement metrics together with likes, remarks, and stocks. These interactions gauge the resonance of your content fabric and its potential to spark sizable conversations.

Click-Through Rate (CTR): Measure CTR to assess the effectiveness of your name-to-movement. CTR presentations the share of customers who clicked in your advert, indicating the quantity of interest generated.

four. Conversion Tracking:

Set Up Conversion Tracking: Implement conversion tracking to degree moves that align collectively together along with your advertising and marketing marketing campaign goals. Whether it's miles completing a purchase, filling out a form, or other favored movements, tracking conversions gives tangible insights into advertising and marketing advertising campaign success.

five.   Return on Ad Spend (ROAS):

ROAS Calculation: Calculate ROAS by the use of manner of dividing the sales generated by means of manner of manner of your classified ads with the aid of the advert spend. This metric offers a easy photo of the pass lower back on funding, assisting you study the profitability of your campaigns.

6.   Click-Through Attribution Models:

Attribution Models: Explore high-quality attribution models to apprehend the consumer adventure. Whether it's miles first-click on on, final-click on on, or multi-touch attribution, choosing the proper model offers insights into the touchpoints contributing to conversions.

7.   Ad Frequency Monitoring:

Frequency Metrics: Keep an eye fixed constant on ad frequency, indicating how frequently customers see your advert. High advert frequency can bring about advert fatigue, and diminishing effectiveness. Rotate advert creatives or modify targeted on to control frequency.

eight. Social Listening and Sentiment Analysis:

Social Listening Tools: Utilize social listening tools to reveal brand mentions, sentiment, and inclinations. Understanding the sentiment round your logo lets in gauge desired perception and pick out out areas for improvement.

User Feedback Analysis: Analyze purchaser remarks and comments in your internet net page. Insights from client interactions offer qualitative information on how your target market perceives and engages collectively with your content material.

9.   Facebook Analytics and Insights:

Utilize Facebook Analytics: Leverage Facebook Analytics for in-intensity insights. Explore individual demographics, net internet page views, and moves taken for your web page. Insights provide a entire evaluate of your target audience and content cloth performance.

10.   A/B Testing for Optimization:

A/B Testing Insights: Apply A/B checking out no longer best to advert innovative but furthermore to goal marketplace targeted on and different variables. Analyzing A/B test effects gives precious insights into what resonates most together together with your target audience and informs future strategies.

11.   Data-Driven Iteration:

Iterative Refinement: Use records to tell iterative refinement. Regularly observe usual overall performance metrics and adjust your method based totally on insights. This statistics-driven technique ensures ongoing optimization and flexibility.

12.   Benchmarking Against Goals:

Compare in opposition to Goals: Benchmark your normal overall performance in opposition to initial desires and dreams. Regularly take a look at whether or not or now not your campaigns are meeting, exceeding, or falling brief of expectancies. Adjust techniques based on those assessments.

thirteen.   Attribution Window Considerations:

Adjust Attribution Windows: Consider the right attribution window in your commercial corporation. Depending in your earnings cycle or conversion course, adjusting the attribution window ensures correct measurement of the impact of your campaigns.

14.   Competitive Analysis:

Competitor Benchmarking: Conduct aggressive analysis to benchmark your ordinary performance towards enterprise pals. Understanding how your metrics check to opposition gives context and highlights regions for development.

Measuring achievement on Facebook is a multifaceted gadget this is going beyond floor-diploma metrics. By embracing a holistic method and constantly refining your techniques based totally mostly on information-pushed insights, you characteristic your logo for sustained boom and impact. In the imminent chapters, we are able to find out advanced methods for goal market engagement and network constructing to further increase your fulfillment at the platform.

6.1 Key Metrics for Facebook Marketing

Understanding and leveraging key metrics is the cornerstone of a a fulfillment Facebook marketing method. In this chapter, we'll discover the essential metrics that offer treasured insights into the overall performance of your campaigns, allowing you to make informed decisions and optimize for success.

1.   Reach:

Definition: Reach measures the pleasant huge sort of customers who've visible your content material material.

Importance: Indicates the size of your goal market and the potential publicity of your content material material.

2.   Impressions:

Definition: Impressions represent the entire huge form of times your content material cloth material is displayed, which include multiple perspectives through the identical customer.

Importance: Provides a complete view of the overall visibility and frequency of your content cloth fabric.

three. Engagement Metrics:

Likes, Comments, Shares:

Likes: The type of users who clicked the "Like" button in your content material fabric.

Comments: The type of purchaser feedback on your posts.

Shares: The sort of instances clients shared your content with their community.

Importance: Measures the amount of interplay and social engagement collectively along with your content material material material.

4.   Click-Through Rate (CTR):

Definition: CTR is the share of customers who clicked to your ad or content material material after seeing it.

Importance: Indicates the effectiveness of your name-to-motion and the relevance of your content material cloth fabric for your target audience.

five.   Conversion Rate:

Definition: Conversion fee measures the proportion of users who finished a favored movement, inclusive of creating a buy or filling out a form, in response for your advert.

Importance: Reflects the success of your campaigns in riding specific actions aligned together collectively together with your goals.

6. Return on Ad Spend (ROAS):

Definition: ROAS calculates the sales generated through your advertisements relative to the advert spend.

Importance: Provides a smooth information of the profitability and performance of your advertising funding.

7. Ad Frequency:

Definition: Ad frequency indicates how frequently customers see your ad.

Importance: High advert frequency can result in ad fatigue, diminishing effectiveness. Monitoring and dealing with advert frequency is important for retaining engagement.

eight. Social Listening and Sentiment Analysis:

Definition: Social listening includes tracking logo mentions and sentiment on social media systems.

Importance: Offers qualitative insights into how your target market perceives your emblem, assisting you apprehend sentiment tendencies and deal with capacity troubles.

nine. Facebook Analytics Metrics:

Page Views, Actions on Page:

Page Views: The amount of instances clients view your Facebook Page.

Actions on Page: Actions taken for your Page, which includes clicks to your cellular phone variety or pointers.

Importance: Provides insights into purchaser interactions and engagement together with your Facebook Page.

10. A/B Testing Insights:

Definition: A/B sorting out entails evaluating versions of an ad or content material to decide which plays higher.

Importance: Offers insights into what resonates most in conjunction with your target marketplace, guiding destiny strategies and optimizations.

eleven.   Video Metrics:

Views, Watch Time, Click-Throughs:

Views: The variety of times your video has been watched.

Watch Time: The general time customers spent looking your video.

Click-Throughs: The variety of clients who clicked on a hyperlink or took motion after searching your video.

Importance: Evaluate the overall performance and engagement of your video content material fabric material.

12.   Click-Through Attribution Models:

Definition: Click-via attribution models characteristic conversions to the very last click on on a person made earlier than taking the desired motion.

Importance: Offers insights into the correct touchpoints that contribute to conversions, supporting in understanding the purchaser journey.

13.   Ad Placement Metrics:

In-Feed Ads, Stories Ads:

In-Feed Ads: Ads that seem in customers' information feeds.

Stories Ads: Full-display commercials in the Stories function.

Importance: Assesses the overall overall performance of commercials in one of a kind placements, guiding strategic choices on wherein to allocate finances.

14.   Competitive Analysis:

Definition: Involves benchmarking your performance in competition to business corporation competition.

Importance: Provides context and highlights areas for improvement through data how your metrics examine to others on your company.

By tracking and decoding the ones key metrics, you advantage precious insights into the effectiveness of your Facebook advertising efforts. Regular evaluation, coupled with records-driven optimizations, ensures that your campaigns are not only visible however additionally impactful. In the approaching chapters, we are able to find out advanced tactics for advertising, aim marketplace engagement, and community building to similarly beautify your Facebook advertising method.

6.2 Analyzing and Adjusting Strategies

Success inside the ever-evolving landscape of Facebook advertising calls for a proactive method to evaluation and non-prevent version. This bankruptcy delves into the vital technique of reading marketing marketing marketing campaign overall performance and making knowledgeable modifications to ensure ongoing achievement.

1.   Regular Performance Audits:

Scheduled Audits: Establish a normal for conducting regular regular overall performance audits. Set specific durations to take a look at key metrics, come to be aware about inclinations, and test the overall effectiveness of your campaigns.

Benchmarking Against Goals: Compare everyday average overall performance in opposition to preliminary dreams and benchmarks. This gives context for evaluating fulfillment and areas for development.

2.   Data-Driven Decision Making:

Metric Prioritization: Prioritize key metrics aligned collectively along with your marketing campaign dreams. Focus on metrics that right now effect your goals, ensuring that your analysis is practical and actionable.

A/B Testing Insights: Leverage A/B trying out insights to inform choice-making. Identify high-acting variables and follow the ones findings to optimize cutting-edge and future campaigns.

3.   Audience Feedback and Sentiment Analysis:

User Comments and Feedback: Analyze consumer feedback and comments for your Facebook Page. Gain qualitative insights into audience sentiment and cope with any problems or questions right away.

Social Listening Tools: Utilize social listening gear to show broader sentiment inclinations. Understand how your emblem is perceived beyond direct interactions on your net internet web page.

Chapter 7: Case Studies

Embarking on a adventure of Facebook marketing is enriched by way of real-international examples that display off strategies in motion. In this financial ruin, we are able to delve into compelling case research that light up a achievement campaigns, supplying precious insights and concept in your non-public endeavors.

1. Campaign: "Engage & Convert" Fitness Apparel Brand:

Objective: Increase online income and logo engagement.

Strategy:

Utilized dynamic advertisements showcasing plenty of merchandise.

Implemented custom audiences based mostly on internet site visits and previous purchases.

A/B examined specific advert creatives and duplicate to optimize engagement.

Results:

Achieved a 30% increase in online earnings.

Boosted engagement with a 20% rise in click on on on-via prices.

Custom goal market targeting induced a 15% growth in conversion costs.

2.   Campaign: "Share the Moment" Travel Agency:

Objective: Enhance emblem recognition and inspire user-generated content material fabric.

Strategy:

Launched a purchaser-generated content material fabric campaign, encouraging customers to percentage journey photographs.

Utilized Facebook Stories and in-feed classified ads to enlarge the campaign.

Incorporated a branded hashtag to foster network engagement.

Results:

Generated a 50% boom in emblem mentions and tagged posts.

Achieved a 25% upward push in logo-related conversations on social media.

Increased ordinary brand popularity with the beneficial resource of 40%.

three. Campaign: "Exclusive Sneak Peek" Tech Product Launch:

Objective: Generate anticipation and pre-orders for a modern day tech product.

Strategy:

Teased the product with specific behind-the-scenes content.

Utilized Facebook Live to unveil capabilities and have interaction with the target market.

Implemented targeted advertisements for pre-order incentives.

Results:

Generated a seventy five% boom in website website site visitors inside the path of the pre-launch period.

Achieved a 50% growth in pre-orders in comparison to preceding launches.

Facebook Live training garnered a 30% boom in aim marketplace engagement.

four. Campaign: "Educate & Convert" Online Learning Platform:

Objective: Drive direction sign-u.S.A. Of americaand engagement.

Strategy:

Developed enticing video content material highlighting course advantages.

Utilized carousel commercials to show off various path offerings.

Targeted custom audiences based totally on customers who regarded path-related pages.

Results:

Achieved a forty% increase in direction sign-ups.

Carousel advertisements delivered about a 25% better click on-via charge.

Custom target market centered on triggered a 20% increase in route completions.

5.   Campaign: "Flash Sale Frenzy" E-trade Fashion Retailer:

Objective: Drive at once income inside the direction of a restrained-time flash sale.

Strategy:

Created a experience of urgency with countdown timers in ad creatives.

Implemented targeted classified ads to precise client segments.

Utilized Facebook Events to promote the flash sale.

Results:

Achieved a 60% increase in income in the direction of the flash sale duration.

Countdown timer advertisements brought about a 35% higher click on on-thru fee.

Facebook Events generated a 25% growth in attendance.

These case studies underscore the power and effectiveness of Facebook advertising and marketing throughout numerous industries. By dissecting a fulfillment campaigns, we glean valuable commands and thoughts that may be carried out to tailor techniques for particular business desires. In the subsequent chapters, we can find out superior techniques for target audience engagement and network constructing, aiming to further elevate your Facebook advertising and marketing and advertising and marketing and marketing and marketing prowess.

7.1 Successful Facebook Marketing Campaigns

In this financial ruin, we are able to find out some of the most a success and impactful Facebook advertising and marketing campaigns that have left an indelible mark at the digital landscape. These campaigns no longer first-rate finished their goals but moreover set new requirements for creativity, engagement, and brand resonance.

1.   Airbnb's "Live There" Campaign:

Objective: Shift notion from excursion inns to immersive community evaluations.

Strategy:

Utilized visually compelling video content material showcasing particular and real journey stories.

Leveraged Facebook's immersive advert codecs, which embody carousel advertisements and Canvas commercials.

Encouraged character-generated content cloth by way of manner of providing tourist tales.

Results:

Achieved a 30% growth in emblem mentions and terrific sentiment.

The advertising and marketing marketing campaign contributed to a 20% beautify in bookings.

User engagement with Airbnb's Facebook internet web page prolonged with the resource of 40%.

2.   Nike's "Breaking2" Initiative:

Objective: Sub-2-hour marathon attempt to expose off innovation and human capability.

Strategy:

Livestreamed the marathon try on Facebook Live, engaging audiences in actual time.

Released teaser content material within the lead-as masses as build anticipation.

Encouraged consumer participation through a committed hashtag.

Results:

Over 13 million web page site visitors tuned in to the Facebook Live event.

The marketing campaign generated top notch media insurance and social media buzz.

Nike's Facebook net web page expert a 25% increase in fans in the direction of the marketing advertising campaign.

three. Coca-Cola's "Share a Coke" Campaign:

Objective: Increase emblem engagement and personalization.

Strategy:

Replaced Coca-Cola emblems with well-known names on product labels.

Encouraged clients to percent personalised bottles on social media.

Implemented focused commercials to attain specific demographics.

Results:

The marketing and advertising advertising campaign caused a 7% boom in profits.

Over 500,000 pix were shared on social media with the #ShareACoke hashtag.

Coca-Cola's Facebook net net web page saw a 50% boom in engagement in some unspecified time in the destiny of the advertising campaign.

4.   Always' "Like a Girl" Empowerment Campaign:

Objective: Challenge stereotypes and empower women and women.

Strategy:

Launched a powerful video difficult the terrible connotations of the word "like a female."

Utilized Facebook's video advert platform to maximise attain.

Encouraged customers to share private stories the use of the advertising and marketing campaign hashtag.

Results:

The video garnered over 90 million views on Facebook.

The hashtag #LikeAGirl trended globally on social media.

The advertising marketing campaign acquired numerous awards for its super effect.

five. Oreo's "Dunk within the Dark" Real-Time Marketing:

Objective: Seize real-time advertising and marketing and advertising possibilities at some stage in the Super Bowl blackout.

Strategy:

Reacted swiftly to the surprising blackout with a clever social media submit.

Leveraged Facebook to percent an photo of an Oreo within the darkish with the caption "You can although dunk within the dark."

Encouraged person engagement through capitalizing on the timely and relevant occasion.

Results:

The placed up went viral, receiving over 20,000 retweets on Twitter and huge Facebook stocks.

Oreo obtained huge media insurance for its short and modern response.

The marketing advertising and marketing marketing campaign exemplified the strength of actual-time advertising and marketing and advertising within the virtual age.

These campaigns characteristic exemplars of progressive and impactful Facebook advertising and marketing. By studying the strategies and consequences of those successes, entrepreneurs can gain treasured insights into powerful strategies, storytelling strategies, and audience engagement techniques. In the subsequent chapters, we are able to discover superior methods for building and nurturing groups on Facebook, fostering lasting connections collectively along with your goal market.

7.2 Learning from Mistakes in Facebook Marketing

While fulfillment stories encourage, getting to know from mistakes is further critical in the journey of Facebook advertising and marketing and advertising. This bankruptcy delves into common pitfalls and missteps encountered through entrepreneurs, providing treasured insights to help you navigate capacity demanding conditions and refine your strategies.

1.   Neglecting Audience Insights:

Mistake: Failing to make use of Facebook's Audience Insights device to understand the target market.

Learning: Regularly leverage Audience Insights to refine focused on, making sure your content material material resonates with the right demographics, hobbies, and behaviors.

2.   Ignoring Mobile Optimization:

Mistake: Overlooking the importance of cell optimization for advert creatives and landing pages.

Learning: Prioritize responsive layout and fast-loading content material for cell customers, acknowledging the maximum critical mobile utilization on Facebook.

3.   Inconsistent Brand Voice:

Mistake: Lack of consistency in logo voice and messaging all through posts and campaigns.

Learning: Establish and preserve a cohesive logo voice, ensuring a unified and recognizable presence that resonates collectively together with your target market.

Chapter 8: Future Trends In Face Book Marketing

As the virtual landscape continues to conform, looking forward to destiny developments is important for staying beforehand inside the realm of Facebook marketing and advertising and advertising and marketing. This bankruptcy explores rising trends and upgrades which may be poised to form the future of advertising and marketing at the platform.

1.   Video Content Dominance:

Trend: The dominance of video content is expected to persist and intensify.

Insight: Marketers should interest on growing appealing and shareable video content material fabric, leveraging functions like Facebook Live for real-time interaction and immersive storytelling.

2.   Augmented Reality (AR) Experiences:

Trend: Increased integration of augmented reality for interactive and customized character opinions.

Insight: Brands can discover AR classified ads and competencies, allowing users to visualize products of their actual-worldwide surroundings, and enhancing the purchasing enjoy.

three. Ephemeral Content on the Rise:

Trend: Growing reputation of ephemeral content material cloth via Stories on Facebook and Instagram.

Insight: Marketers want to leverage the temporary nature of Stories for real, inside the back of-the-scenes content material cloth and time-touchy promotions.

4. Conversational Marketing with Chatbots:

Trend: Widespread use of chatbots for customized and automated customer interactions.

Insight: Implement chatbots on Facebook Messenger for instant customer service, lead technology, and guiding customers thru the earnings funnel.

5.   Social Commerce Integration:

Trend: The integration of e-change features at once inner social media structures.

Insight: Brands can optimize their Facebook presence for seamless buying evaluations, such as in-app purchases and direct product showcases.

6.   Personalization through AI:

Trend: Increasing use of artificial intelligence (AI) for customized content fabric tips.

Insight: Marketers can leverage AI algorithms to investigate individual behavior and alternatives, turning in tailored content cloth and commercials.

7.   User-Generated Content Amplification:

Trend: Continued emphasis on consumer-generated content cloth as a powerful advertising and advertising device.

Insight: Encourage customers to create and share content material material associated with your emblem, fostering authenticity and network engagement.

eight. Privacy-Centric Marketing:

Trend: Growing significance of privateness worries in advertising strategies.

Insight: Marketers want to prioritize obvious facts practices, gain character consent, and adhere to evolving privacy guidelines to construct and hold agree with.

nine.   Integration of Social Causes:

Trend: Increased emphasis on brands aligning with social reasons and values.

Insight: Incorporate reason-driven advertising, showcasing social responsibility, and network involvement to resonate with socially conscious audiences.

10. Multi-Channel Marketing Integration:

Trend: A shift towards protected multi-channel advertising and marketing and marketing strategies.

Insight: Marketers need to create cohesive campaigns within the path of various structures, aligning messaging and visuals for a unified emblem enjoy.

eleven. Virtual and Augmented Reality Advertising:

Trend: Growing exploration of virtual and augmented reality for advertising abilties.

Insight: Brands can check with immersive advert reviews, supplying users a greater interactive and appealing manner to connect to products or services.

12. Voice Search Optimization:

Trend: The rise of voice-activated gadgets influencing are attempting to find conduct.

Insight: Optimize content material material cloth for voice trying to find, ensuring that your emblem stays discoverable as voice interactions become extra well-known.

As Facebook marketing and marketing evolves, staying attuned to the ones future tendencies empowers entrepreneurs to conform techniques, capitalize on growing opportunities, and keep a dynamic and effective presence on the platform. In the subsequent chapters, we will discover advanced strategies for community building, goal market engagement, and cultivating logo advocates on Facebook.

nine.1 Emerging Technologies and Strategies

In the ever-evolving landscape of digital advertising, staying beforehand requires a keen eye on growing era and progressive techniques. This financial disaster explores cutting-edge technology and ahead-thinking techniques which can be reshaping the destiny of Facebook advertising and advertising.

1. Artificial Intelligence (AI) and Machine Learning:

Technology: AI and machine reading algorithms for stronger targeted on and personalization.

Strategy: Implement AI-pushed equipment to analyze man or woman behavior, are waiting for alternatives, and supply exceptionally personalised content material and classified ads.

2. Augmented Reality (AR) Advertising:

Technology: Integration of AR for interactive and immersive ad studies.

Strategy: Explore AR advertising formats, permitting users to have interaction with merchandise in actual-worldwide environments, enhancing the overall buying revel in.

3. Virtual Reality (VR) Experiences:

Technology: VR generation for growing immersive emblem reports.

Strategy: Experiment with VR content material cloth material, permitting customers to in fact discover merchandise, environments, or sports, fostering a deeper reference to the brand.

4. Chatbots and Conversational Marketing:

Technology: Advanced chatbots powered thru natural language processing.

Strategy: Deploy chatbots on Facebook Messenger for actual-time consumer interactions, lead era, and guiding users via the patron adventure.

five. Blockchain for Transparency and Security:

Technology: Blockchain for apparent and consistent transactions.

Strategy: Explore blockchain packages to beautify transparency in advertising and marketing and advertising, making sure sincere interactions and statistics protection.

6. 360-degree Video and Immersive Storytelling:

Technology: 360-degree video generation for immersive storytelling.

Strategy: Leverage 360-degree movies on Facebook to create charming and interactive narratives, presenting clients with a more attractive logo revel in.

7. Social Commerce Integrations:

Technology: Seamless integration of e-exchange skills interior social media structures.

Strategy: Optimize Facebook for social alternate, permitting clients to make purchases right now at the platform, and streamlining the route from discovery to conversion.

eight. Voice Search Optimization:

Technology: Voice-activated devices and voice search technology.

Strategy: Optimize content material cloth for voice are seeking for, ensuring that manufacturers live discoverable as voice interactions emerge as more and more everyday.

nine. Predictive Analytics for Customer Insights:

Technology: Predictive analytics models for watching for individual conduct.

Strategy: Utilize predictive analytics to expect man or woman options, allowing extra proactive and custom designed advertising strategies.

10. Social Listening Tools and Sentiment Analysis:

Technology: Advanced social listening tools with sentiment assessment abilities.

Strategy: Employ those gadget to expose logo mentions, sentiment, and developments, gaining treasured insights into aim market perceptions and options.

eleven.   5G   Technology   and   Faster
Loading Times:

Technology: The   introduction   of   5G
generation for quicker internet speeds.

Strategy: Optimize content cloth for faster
loading   instances,   capitalizing   on   5G
competencies   to   deliver   seamless   and
attractive patron opinions.

12.   Dynamic and Interactive Content:

Technology: Dynamic content formats and
interactive factors.

Strategy: Experiment with dynamic classified
ads and interactive content material fabric to
capture purchaser interest and inspire lively
engagement.

By embracing those rising generation and
integrating in advance-questioning strategies,
marketers can feature themselves on the
main fringe of innovation in Facebook
advertising and advertising. As we go with the
flow forward, the subsequent chapters will

delve into superior techniques for community building, intention market engagement, and cultivating brand advocates on Facebook.

nine.2 Adapting to Changes inside the Social Media Landscape

Navigating the dynamic terrain of social media requires entrepreneurs to be agile and aware of adjustments. This financial disaster explores techniques for adapting to shifts inside the social media landscape, ensuring that your Facebook advertising efforts stay effective and relevant.

1.   Continuous Platform Monitoring:

Approach: Regularly display screen updates, talents, and set of rules changes on Facebook and exclusive applicable structures.

Strategy: Stay informed about the evolving social media landscape to proactively adjust your strategies based at the modern-day day platform dynamics.

2.   Flexibility in Content Strategies:

Approach: Build flexibility into your content material fabric techniques.

Strategy: Be organized to pivot content material mission topics, codecs, and posting frequencies based totally on the changing options and behaviors of your target market.

three. Embrace New Features and Formats:

Approach: Actively find out and include new abilities and codecs offered with the useful useful resource of social media structures.

Strategy: Experiment with rising functions on Facebook, together with stay video, Stories, or augmented fact, to live earlier of dispositions and seize target audience hobby.

four. Data-Driven Decision-Making:

Approach: Base alternatives on complete facts evaluation.

Strategy: Regularly evaluation fashionable performance metrics, purchaser engagement, and goal marketplace insights to tell modifications to your Facebook advertising and marketing technique.

5.   Community   Engagement   and Feedback:

Approach: Foster open communique together with your target marketplace.

Strategy: Encourage comments, respond to feedback, and actively have interaction together with your community to construct a responsive and linked on line presence.

6.   Diversification of Platforms:

Approach: Avoid reliance on a single social media platform.

Strategy: Diversify your on line presence at some point of a couple of structures, ensuring that modifications on one platform do now not disproportionately effect your normal virtual strategy.

7.   Agility in Ad Campaigns:

Approach: Design campaigns with agility in mind.

Strategy: Plan campaigns that may be without issues adjusted or scaled based totally on real-time overall performance, bearing in thoughts brief variations as wanted.

eight. Collaboration with Influencers:

Approach: Cultivate relationships with influencers to your business enterprise.

Strategy: Collaborate with influencers for campaigns and promotions, leveraging their potential to reach and engage unique intention marketplace segments.

nine. User Privacy and Data Ethics:

Approach: Prioritize client privacy and ethical records practices.

Strategy: Stay abreast of privacy guidelines, advantage client consent, and communicate transparently approximately information dealing with to assemble and hold don't forget.

10. Crisis Management Preparedness:

Approach: Develop a catastrophe control plan.

Strategy: Be organized to respond hastily and as it need to be to any unforeseen disturbing conditions, collectively with horrible publicity or social media backlash.

11. Industry and Trend Monitoring:

Approach: Keep a finger on the pulse of industry trends.

Strategy: Monitor enterprise dispositions and tendencies to make certain that your Facebook advertising strategies align with contemporary-day market dynamics and patron expectations.

12. Employee Training and Skill Development:

Approach: Invest in non-prevent training in your advertising and advertising and advertising company.

Strategy: Equip your business enterprise with the capabilities needed to adapt to new generation, structures, and advertising inclinations, fostering a lifestyle of mastering and innovation.

Adapting to modifications inside the social media landscape is a strategic essential for sustained achievement in Facebook marketing and marketing. By staying vigilant, final records-pushed, and embracing a way of life of adaptability, entrepreneurs can not most effective weather modifications however furthermore capitalize on growing opportunities within the ever-evolving worldwide of social media. In the approaching chapters, we are able to delve into advanced techniques for goal market engagement, network constructing, and brand advocacy on Facebook.

Chapter 9: Stand E-Book Advertising

Understanding the Power of Face book for Local Businesses

In current virtual age, social media has grow to be an vital a part of our everyday lives. Among the numerous systems to be had, Face book stands out as one of the most effective equipment for local businesses to connect to their goal marketplace and increase their on-line presence. This subchapter targets to shed moderate at the massive strength of Face book for nearby companies, emphasizing why it is essential for them to encompass Face book advertising and marketing and advertising as a part of their normal marketing method.

Face book boasts an outstanding kind of lively customers, making it a really best platform for organizations to acquire a huge target audience. With over 2.Eight billion monthly active customers globally, it gives a superb pool of functionality customers proper at your fingertips. By tapping into this consumer base, nearby agencies can increase their accumulate beyond their bodily place and purpose clients of their close by businesses and beyond.

One of the vital element advantages of Face book for nearby organizations is its capability to goal unique demographics and pursuits. Through Face book's advanced targeted on alternatives, agencies can create highly tailor-made advertisements that attain the right humans at the right time. Whether it's age, gender, vicinity, or pastimes, Facebook's focused on abilities allow organizations to maximize their advertising efforts and make certain that their message is attaining the right target marketplace.

Moreover, Facebook offers a whole lot of tools and functions designed particularly for community agencies. Features inclusive of Facebook Pages, Groups, and Events permit agencies to engage with their clients on a extra private degree, fostering a enjoy of community and loyalty. By developing and keeping an active Facebook presence, groups can display off their products or services, percentage updates and promotions, and at once have interaction with clients via feedback, messages, and opinions.

Furthermore, Facebook's marketing and advertising platform offers severa advert codecs, collectively with picture advertisements, video classified ads, carousel classified ads, and further. This versatility allows organizations to check with particular codecs and discover the best way to seize their target audience's interest. Additionally, Facebook's strong analytics and insights offer companies with precious information on their ad common common performance, helping them refine their strategies and optimize their marketing and marketing and advertising campaigns.

In give up, Facebook's strength for nearby companies cannot be overstated. From its extensive character base to its advanced centered on competencies and specialised tools, Facebook gives close by agencies a totally specific possibility to growth their accumulate, have interaction with their aim market, and growth their logo visibility. By mastering Facebook advertising and marketing, community corporations can tap into the tremendous capability of this platform and lift their online presence to new heights.

Benefits of Utilizing Facebook Marketing for Local Businesses

In modern digital age, social media has become an vital tool for companies, specifically close to carrying out out to community clients. Among the numerous social media systems to be had, Facebook stands proud as a effective advertising device that may assist neighborhood organizations hook up with their goal marketplace and improve their boom. This subchapter desires to consciousness at the numerous advantages of the use of Facebook advertising and marketing for neighborhood companies.

1. Enhanced brand consciousness: Facebook lets in community agencies to create and maintain a strong on line presence. By often posting engaging content fabric, businesses can increase their brand visibility and gain a far wider audience internal their network network. This improved publicity permits to set up credibility and consider, making it much less complicated for customers to pick out your organisation over competition.

2. Targeted advertising and advertising and marketing: Facebook's superior centered on alternatives allow network companies to create quite precise advertising campaigns. By deciding on demographics, pastimes, and behaviors, corporations can make certain that their classified ads are shown to the most applicable target marketplace. This centered method not best will boom the possibilities of conversion but additionally saves cash thru doing away with wasted advert spend on beside the factor audiences.

3. Cost-powerful marketing: Compared to traditional marketing techniques, Facebook advertising is considerably extra cost-effective. Even with a limited finances, nearby businesses can create enticing content fabric, run focused advertisements, and degree the move again on funding (ROI) via Facebook's analytics gear. This makes Facebook advertising an super alternative for small corporations trying to maximize their advertising and marketing and advertising efforts.

4. Improved patron engagement: Facebook gives an interactive platform for neighborhood groups to have interaction with their customers. By responding to remarks, messages, and opinions, companies can construct strong relationships and exhibit superb customer service. This level of engagement no longer simplest enhances patron pride but moreover encourages super phrase-of-mouth referrals, most important to elevated emblem loyalty and repeat commercial organisation.

five. Access to precious insights: Facebook's analytics tools offer neighborhood companies with actionable insights about their target audience, content material widespread overall performance, and marketing and advertising campaigns. By analyzing those metrics, businesses can choose out dispositions, recognize consumer choices, and refine their advertising and marketing techniques consequently. This statistics-driven method enables corporations make informed alternatives, resulting in more effective advertising and advertising efforts.

In give up, Facebook advertising offers a plethora of benefits for nearby organizations. From extended brand interest and targeted advertising and advertising and marketing to fee-effective advertising and advanced purchaser engagement, utilising Facebook as a advertising tool can drastically beautify the growth and success of close by companies. By leveraging the energy of Facebook, groups can connect with their close by goal market, power site visitors, and ultimately growth income, ensuring prolonged-time period achievement in an ever-evolving digital panorama.

Common Challenges Faced by means of using manner of Local Businesses on Facebook

In present day virtual age, having a robust on line presence is essential for the achievement of any close by commercial business enterprise. With over 2.8 billion month-to-month active customers, Facebook has turn out to be an critical platform for agencies to hook up with their goal market. However, navigating the complexities of Facebook advertising and marketing and advertising can be a frightening undertaking. In this subchapter, we are capable of explore the commonplace challenges confronted via nearby agencies on Facebook and provide sensible solutions to overcome them.

One of the essential annoying conditions community organizations face on Facebook is competition. With so many organizations vying for the eye of clients, repute out from the group can be hard. It is vital to growth a completely particular brand voice and create appealing content material material that resonates at the side of your goal marketplace. Understanding your clients' goals and alternatives will assist you tailor your content material technique to satisfy their expectancies.

Another undertaking is the consistent adjustments in Facebook's algorithms and suggestions. As the platform evolves, businesses should live updated with the stylish changes to make certain their content material reaches their audience. Regularly monitoring Facebook's updates and adapting your advertising and advertising strategies consequently will assist you live beforehand of the curve.

Finding the proper balance amongst natural and paid benefit is also a commonplace undertaking. While natural achieve allows you to hook up with your present fans, paid advertising will let you achieve a much wider intention marketplace. It is critical to allocate a fee variety for Facebook advertisements and punctiliously motive your audience to maximize the go back on funding.

Engaging along with your intention marketplace and managing patron comments is some different mission close by businesses face on Facebook. Responding to client inquiries and proceedings in a nicely timed and professional way is essential for preserving a effective brand photograph. Implementing a social media control device can streamline this technique and assist you efficiently manipulate your on line interactions.

Lastly, measuring the achievement of your Facebook advertising efforts may be hard. It is vital to set smooth goals and song key conventional typical performance signs (KPIs) to evaluate the effectiveness of your strategies. Utilizing Facebook Insights and certainly one of a type analytics equipment can provide treasured insights into patron behavior and help you're making information-pushed alternatives.

In stop, on the equal time as Facebook advertising and marketing and advertising and marketing and advertising for close by businesses can pose numerous annoying situations, with the proper techniques and equipment, you could triumph over them and obtain fulfillment. By information your target market, staying updated with Facebook's adjustments, balancing herbal and paid gather, engaging collectively collectively along with your target market, and measuring your traditional typical overall performance, you can hold near Facebook advertising and strength increase for your local commercial enterprise enterprise.

Setting Realistic Goals for Your Facebook Marketing Strategy

When it involves Facebook advertising for close by corporations, it's miles essential to set sensible dreams that align collectively together with your contemporary advertising and advertising method. Without easy objectives in mind, your efforts at the platform may be scattered and ineffective. In this subchapter, we're capable of discover the importance of placing realistic goals to your Facebook marketing method and provide you with actionable steps that will help you reap success.

Why Set Realistic Goals?

Setting sensible goals is crucial for any close by business enterprise searching for to make an impact on Facebook. It lets in you to attention your efforts, measure your improvement, and adjust your technique therefore. By putting in place particular dreams, you could higher apprehend the effectiveness of your campaigns and make facts-driven choices to optimize your advertising and marketing efforts.

Chapter 10: Face Book Marketing Strategy

Defining Your Target Audience and Buyer Persona

In modern-day virtual age, Facebook has become an essential device for nearby groups looking to connect to their target market and energy earnings. However, an amazing way to make the most from your Facebook advertising and advertising and marketing efforts, it's miles essential to first define your goal marketplace and create a patron character.

Your purpose market is the precise agency of humans that your services or products are designed for. By figuring out and expertise your target marketplace, you could tailor your marketing and advertising messages and strategies to resonate with their desires and possibilities. This will ultimately result in extra powerful and a success Facebook advertising and marketing campaigns.

To define your audience, start via reading your present patron base. Look for not unusual trends together with age, gender, area, interests, and buying behaviors. This facts will provide treasured insights into the form of parents which might be maximum likely to be inquisitive about what your local business organisation has to provide.

Once you've got were given a clean understanding of your target audience, it's time to create a patron character. A customer individual is an extensive profile of your exceptional patron. It is going past demographic statistics and delves into their motivations, worrying situations, and dreams. By creating a consumer man or woman, you can higher apprehend the attitude of your purpose marketplace and tailor your advertising and advertising messages as a end result.

When growing a purchaser character, keep in mind factors together with their job name, earnings degree, own family reputation, hobbies, and pain factors. For instance, if you are a community bakery, your patron individual can be a busy working determine who values comfort and wholesome snacks for their youngsters.

Having a properly-defined customer personality will assist you craft compelling Facebook commercials, create attractive content, and provide treasured solutions for your target market's issues. It will guide your advertising and advertising alternatives and make sure which you are accomplishing the right humans collectively along with your Facebook marketing efforts.

In surrender, defining your audience and developing a consumer man or woman is a important step in getting to know Facebook advertising and marketing for neighborhood agencies. By statistics who your first-class customers are and what motivates them, you can create rather targeted and effective marketing campaigns that stress results. So make the effort to research and outline your target audience and customer personality, and watch your Facebook advertising efforts soar to new heights.

Developing a Compelling Brand Story

In contemporary-day especially aggressive enterprise panorama, having a compelling brand story is essential for community agencies trying to thrive on Facebook. Your logo tale is the narrative that defines your business corporation, creates an emotional reference to your target audience, and devices you aside from your competitors. It is the key to constructing consider, loyalty, and in the long run driving earnings. In this subchapter, we are capable of discover the important factors of developing a compelling logo story and a way to efficiently talk it on Facebook.

The first step in crafting your logo story is to define your logo's identity. What values, challenge, and vision does your organization encompass? What makes you unique? Understanding the ones factors will assist you create an real and relatable story that resonates along facet your target marketplace. Whether it is your dedication to sustainability, your nearby roots, or your incredible customer service, pick out the center elements that make your business organization stand out.

Once you have got were given described your emblem's identity, it's time to create a story that brings it to existence. Your tale have to be attractive, memorable, and aligned together together with your intention marketplace's goals and desires. Think about the annoying situations your clients face and the way your industrial company can provide solutions. Use storytelling techniques to captivate your target audience, which includes sharing personal anecdotes, customer success memories, or at the back of-the-scenes glimpses of your commercial business enterprise.

Facebook offers severa system to efficiently talk your emblem tale. Utilize exquisite visuals, in conjunction with pics and films, to expose off your products, offerings, and the people in the returned of your logo. Create attractive posts that inform reminiscences, evoke emotions, and encourage interplay. Leverage Facebook Live to host digital sports, percentage tutorials, or deliver your goal market an indoors have a look at your industrial agency. Remember to constantly align your content material fabric fabric collectively along side your logo's values and challenge.

To maximize the effect of your brand story on Facebook, do not forget leveraging purchaser-generated content material fabric. Encourage your customers to percentage their reminiscences together together with your emblem and reshare their posts for your internet web page. This now not simplest strengthens the authenticity of your tale however furthermore fosters a revel in of community and take delivery of as proper with amongst your target marketplace.

In cease, developing a compelling logo story is critical for nearby corporations searching for to attain achievement on Facebook. By defining your emblem's identity, developing a captivating narrative, and the use of Facebook's tool correctly, you could construct a strong emotional connection with your goal marketplace. Remember, your emblem story isn't only a advertising and marketing and advertising device; it's far the coronary heart and soul of your business enterprise that units you aside inside the aggressive global of Facebook advertising and marketing and advertising and marketing.

Optimizing Your Facebook Business Page

In contemporary virtual age, having a sturdy on-line presence is essential for close by agencies to thrive. And on the subject of social media marketing, Facebook stays the undisputed king. With over 2.Eight billion monthly energetic customers, it gives an exquisite platform for close by organizations to connect to their target audience. However, definitely having a Facebook Business Page isn't always sufficient. To absolutely harness the energy of Facebook advertising, close by groups need to optimize their business internet web web page effectively. This subchapter will guide you via the system of optimizing your Facebook Business Page for optimum engagement and success.

First and essential, it is crucial to make certain that your Facebook Business Page is whole and up to date. Provide correct data approximately your business commercial enterprise organisation, consisting of deal with, phone variety, hours of operation, and a compelling description that captures the essence of your brand. Remember, your Facebook Business Page acts as a digital storefront, so make sure it leaves a protracted-lasting effect.

Next, consciousness on creating exceptional and visually appealing content material material material. Visuals are vital in taking snap shots the eye of your purpose marketplace. Use adorable pictures, movies, and images that replicate your brand's character and resonate along facet your intention market. Remember to optimize your visuals for cellular devices, as most customers get right of access to Facebook from their smartphones.

Furthermore, interact at the side of your target audience regularly. Respond immediately to remarks, messages, and evaluations to show your clients that you fee their feedback and are dedicated to providing superb customer support. Encourage customers to go away reviews, as superb critiques can substantially have an impact on capability customers' preference-making approach.

Another vital aspect of optimizing your Facebook Business Page is leveraging Facebook's capabilities and device. Take benefit of the selection-to-motion button to pressure particular movements, which incorporates booking an appointment or developing a buy. Utilize Facebook Insights to advantage treasured insights into your target audience's demographics, options, and engagement metrics. This information will assist you refine your marketing and advertising and marketing strategies and create content material that resonates collectively with your audience.

Lastly, don't forget to combine your Facebook Business Page with other advertising and marketing channels. Cross-promote your Facebook presence in your website, e-mail newsletters, and precise social media systems. This will make certain a constant and cohesive brand enjoy on your goal marketplace.

Optimizing your Facebook Business Page calls for time, attempt, and a deep expertise of your target marketplace. However, by following those strategies, you could maximize your Facebook advertising and marketing efforts and installation a robust on-line presence to your network commercial corporation. Stay tuned for the following financial ruin, in which we will delve deeper into superior Facebook advertising techniques tailored particularly for neighborhood organizations.

Crafting Engaging Content for Local Customers

In current-day virtual age, Facebook has emerge as an essential platform for nearby corporations looking to connect with their intention marketplace. With billions of active clients, Facebook presents an terrific opportunity to reach and have interaction with functionality clients in your nearby network. However, to absolutely harness the electricity of Facebook advertising, nearby groups want to discover ways to craft engaging content that resonates with their target market.

Understanding your nearby customers is essential to growing compelling content material fabric that captures their interest and drives them to achieve this. Start through carrying out thorough market studies to perceive the demographics, hobbies, and behaviors of your target marketplace. This information will lay the foundation in your content method, permitting you to tailor your messages to their precise dreams and options.

When crafting content fabric for Facebook, it's far crucial to strike a balance amongst promotional and value-pushed posts. While it is tempting to continuously sell your services or products, excessive self-vending can alienate your audience. Instead, hobby on imparting treasured and applicable content cloth that educates, entertains, or solves a problem for your community customers. For example, a neighborhood bakery also can need to percentage recipes, baking suggestions, or inside the lower back of-the-scenes memories to have interaction their target marketplace and show off their facts.

Visual content fabric cloth is mainly effective on Facebook, because it has a bent to capture hobby and generate better stages of engagement. Incorporate desirable pictures, films, infographics, or maybe live streams into your content approach to captivate your close by target audience. Be best to optimize your visuals for cell, as the majority of Facebook customers get proper of access to the platform from their smartphones.

Another effective technique for attractive community customers is to encourage patron-generated content material cloth. By asking your customers to percentage their studies, critiques, or photos related to your commercial organisation, you create a experience of community and authenticity. This no longer simplest boosts engagement but moreover complements your logo's credibility and social proof.

Lastly, recall to display screen and study the overall overall performance of your content material material fabric regularly. Facebook Insights offers precious facts on acquire, engagement, and audience demographics, allowing you to refine your content cloth material approach over the years. Pay interest to the sorts of content material that resonate most in conjunction with your local customers, and adjust your technique consequently.

Crafting attractive content material fabric cloth for nearby customers on Facebook is a non-forestall technique of experimentation and refinement. By expertise your goal market, offering rate, incorporating seen factors, encouraging man or woman-generated content material fabric, and reading your results, you may draw close Facebook advertising and advertising on your network industrial business company and set up a sturdy online presence inner your community.

Chapter 11: Building And Growing

Building a Strong Facebook Following for Your Local Business

In extraordinarily-modern virtual age, Facebook has emerge as an important device for community organizations to hook up with their target audience and pressure boom. With billions of lively customers, it is a platform that can't be omitted with regards to advertising and marketing your neighborhood enterprise. This subchapter will manual you thru the way of building a robust Facebook following for your community enterprise business enterprise, making sure that you are maximizing your on-line presence and achieving your goal market efficaciously.

Firstly, it's far crucial to recognize your purpose market and their options. Research and have a look at your superb purchaser profile. Who are they? What are their pursuits? By facts your goal marketplace, you may tailor your content fabric to resonate with them and create attractive posts that lure their interest.

Consistency is prime almost about building a robust Facebook following. Develop a content material material approach that consists of a mixture of informative, appealing, and promotional content. Regularly placed up updates, gives, and activities to preserve your target marketplace engaged and interested by your agency. Aim for at the least 3 to five posts in keeping with week to maintain a everyday presence.

Quality over quantity is a few different vital factor of building a sturdy Facebook following. Ensure that your content material is nicely-written, visually appealing, and applicable for your target market. Use beautiful images, videos, and infographics to capture interest and growth engagement. Remember to encompass a name-to-movement to your posts to encourage your target audience to like, remark, and percentage your content material.

Engagement is the lifeblood of Facebook advertising and marketing. Respond to comments and messages directly, displaying your target market that you price their input and are aware of their needs. Encourage conversations via the use of asking questions or website hosting contests. By fostering engagement, you could build a committed community round your community organisation.

Facebook classified ads can be a powerful device to reinforce your following and obtain a far broader aim market. Experiment with unique ad codecs, targeted on alternatives, and budgets to find what works wonderful to your commercial enterprise employer. Consider walking campaigns that sell top notch offers or discounts to entice humans to love and have a look at your net web page.

Lastly, song your development and have a look at the effects of your Facebook marketing and advertising efforts. Utilize Facebook Insights to evaluate the overall

overall overall performance of your posts and commercials, and make data-pushed alternatives to optimize your method in addition.

By implementing the ones strategies, you can collect a strong Facebook following in your close by commercial enterprise, increase brand awareness, and ultimately force greater customers through your doors. Facebook advertising and marketing for close by businesses is a dynamic and ever-evolving subject, so live up to date with the cutting-edge traits and keep to adapt your technique to stay in advance of the competition.

Engaging with Your Facebook Community

Building a robust and engaged community on Facebook is critical for nearby companies on the lookout for to maximize their online presence and lift patron loyalty. In this subchapter, we're able to discover effective techniques and extremely good practices for attractive collectively together along with your Facebook community, helping you connect to your purpose market, foster vast relationships, and force commercial enterprise increase.

1. Create Compelling Content:

To have interaction your Facebook network, it is essential to offer treasured and relevant content fabric that resonates together with your audience. Share informative articles, enterprise information, useful recommendations, and behind-the-scenes glimpses into your industrial corporation. Use hobby-grabbing headlines, captivating visuals, and compelling storytelling strategies to capture your lovers' interest.

2. Encourage Conversations:

acebook is all about interplay, so make sure to ask questions, create polls, and inspire discussions amongst your network individuals. Respond right away and in reality to comments and messages, fostering a experience of open communication and making your target market experience heard and valued. Building a two-manner verbal exchange will make stronger the bond among your business enterprise and your customers.

three. Run Contests and Giveaways:

Contests and giveaways are exceptional gear to have interaction along with your Facebook community and generate pleasure. Whether it is a picture contest, a caption opposition, or a random draw, create opportunities on your enthusiasts to take part and win. Encourage them to percent their reviews, pics, and mind related to your business, similarly improving engagement and growing your attain.

four. Show Appreciation:

Demonstrate your gratitude inside the path of your Facebook community thru way of spotting and highlighting dependable clients, network members, or influencers who guide your business enterprise. Share their stories, testimonials, or man or woman-generated content material cloth, showcasing their excellent opinions. This not quality makes them feel preferred but additionally encourages others to have interaction and proportion their non-public reviews.

five. Utilize Facebook Groups:

Consider developing or joining applicable Facebook agencies associated with your region of hobby or localized community. These companies offer an superb platform to have interaction with like-minded individuals, share business enterprise insights, and establish your self as a knowledgeable useful resource. Actively participate in discussions, provide treasured recommendation, and sell your agency at the same time as suitable, ensuring a immoderate exceptional and useful presence inside the community.

By actively attractive together together with your Facebook community, you could construct robust relationships, foster brand advocacy, and stress natural boom in your community commercial enterprise. Remember to continuously show your metrics, observe the fulfillment of your engagement techniques, and adapt based in your intention marketplace's options and goals. Mastering the paintings of community engagement on Facebook will really help your community business corporation flourish in the ever-evolving virtual panorama.

Encouraging User-Generated Content and Reviews

In latest digital age, harnessing the electricity of consumer-generated content and critiques is crucial for nearby agencies seeking to maximize their presence on Facebook. User-generated content refers to any form of content, which include photographs, motion pictures, or testimonials, that is created through clients and shared on social media systems. These authentic and actual pieces of content can drastically effect a neighborhood commercial enterprise's on line reputation and attract new customers. In this subchapter, we can explore strategies and pleasant practices for encouraging consumer-generated content material and reviews on

Facebook, ultimately helping nearby groups thrive in the aggressive digital panorama.

1. Create an Engaging and Shareable Experience: To encourage users to generate content related to your enterprise, it is important to provide them with an extraordinary revel in really worth sharing. Ensure that your products or services are of high quality, and your customer support is top-notch. When clients have a advantageous revel in, they're more likely to share their thoughts and suggestions on Facebook.

2. Implement Call-to-Actions: Explicitly ask your customers to leave reviews or share their reviews on Facebook. Include call-to-movements in your advertising materials, website, and even in-shop signage. By making it clear and easy for clients to leave a evaluate, you are much more likely to obtain person-generated content.

3. Engage with User-Generated Content: When clients take the time to create content or go away reviews approximately your

business, ensure to have interaction with them. Respond to their posts, comments, and messages to reveal your appreciation and build a sense of community. By engaging with person-generated content, you inspire others to participate and contribute as well.

4. Run Contests and Giveaways: Contests and giveaways are an first-rate way to inspire customers to generate content material. Encourage customers to share their stories or create content related to your enterprise for a threat to win a prize. This no longer best generates person-generated content material but also increases brand cognizance and engagement.

Chapter 12: Mastering Face Book Advertising For Local Businesses

Understanding Facebook Ads Manager and Its Features

In today's virtual age, Facebook has emerge as an essential platform for local businesses to attain and have interaction with their target audience. With over 2.Eight billion monthly lively customers, Facebook offers a vast potential marketplace for agencies of all sizes. However, correctly harnessing the electricity of Facebook advertising and marketing requires a deep expertise of its gear and functions.

One such device that nearby organizations can leverage is the Facebook Ads Manager. This powerful platform permits businesses to create, manipulate, and optimize their advertising and marketing campaigns on Facebook. By learning the usage of Facebook Ads Manager, neighborhood groups can enhance their online presence, growth logo recognition, and pressure more traffic to their web sites.

Facebook Ads Manager offers a extensive range of features that permit groups to create rather targeted and personalized advert campaigns. One of the important thing features is audience concentrated on, which permits agencies to outline their best target market based totally on demographics, hobbies, and behaviors. This guarantees that advertisements are proven to the most applicable customers, maximizing the possibilities of engagement and conversion.

Another important characteristic of Facebook Ads Manager is ad innovative customization. Businesses can choose from a number of advert codecs, which includes single photographs, movies, carousels, and slideshows, to create visually attractive and tasty commercials. Additionally, businesses can add compelling advert replica and make contact with-to-action buttons to set off users to take the favored action, consisting of making a purchase or signing up for a e-newsletter.

Furthermore, Facebook Ads Manager gives strong monitoring and analytics skills. Businesses can tune the performance in their advertisements in actual-time, display key metrics along with reach, impressions, clicks, and conversions, and make data-driven choices to optimize their campaigns. This permits agencies to perceive what works and what does not, and constantly refine their advertising strategies for higher consequences.

To make the most of Facebook Ads Manager, local organizations should also explore advanced functions such as lookalike audiences, which help locate new capacity customers with similar characteristics to their current patron base. Additionally, organizations can make use of retargeting to re-have interaction with users who've formerly interacted with their ads or website, increasing the possibilities of conversion.

In end, understanding and efficiently making use of Facebook Ads Manager is essential for nearby groups seeking to reach Facebook advertising. By harnessing its capabilities consisting of audience targeting, ad innovative customization, and monitoring and analytics, agencies can create notably focused and tasty ad campaigns, drive greater visitors, and ultimately boost their revenue. Mastery of Facebook Ads Manager is a valuable skill that may deliver neighborhood agencies a aggressive area within the ever-evolving virtual panorama.

Defining Your Advertising Objectives and Budget

In cutting-edge digital age, Facebook advertising and marketing has emerge as an crucial tool for nearby agencies seeking to reach a wider target audience and enhance their online presence. However, before diving into the sector of Facebook advertising, it is crucial to define your advertising targets and budget to make sure a a hit and fee-effective campaign.

Setting clean advertising targets is step one closer to developing a centered and centered Facebook advertising strategy. Ask yourself, what do you hope to obtain through your marketing efforts? Are you seeking to increase emblem focus, drive extra traffic on your internet site, generate leads, or sell a specific product or service? Identifying your goals will help you tailor your Facebook ads to meet these objectives.

Once you have got defined your advertising targets, the next step is to establish a realistic budget. Allocating the right quantity of funds on your Facebook marketing campaign is essential for maximizing its effectiveness. Consider your common marketing finances and determine how a great deal you're inclined to put money into Facebook advertising. It's crucial to strike a balance between spending sufficient to gain your goals at the same time as heading off overspending.

When figuring out your price range, recall different factors consisting of your target market length, the competitiveness of your industry, and the duration of your marketing campaign. Facebook gives specific marketing options, which include fee-according to-click (CPC) and cost-according to-influence (CPM), which assist you to manipulate your spending and optimize your finances based on your objectives.

Additionally, bear in mind the lifetime value (LTV) of your customers when placing your Facebook advertising budget. If your business relies on repeat customers or lengthy-time period relationships, investing greater in customer acquisition via Facebook commercials might be profitable.

Remember, tracking and evaluating your Facebook marketing performance is important to understanding its effectiveness. Regularly analyze key metrics consisting of click-thru quotes (CTR), conversion prices, and return on ad spend (ROAS) to measure the success of your campaigns. This statistics allow you to refine your advertising goals and regulate your budget for this reason to obtain higher consequences.

In conclusion, defining your advertising targets and price range is a essential first step in learning Facebook marketing for neighborhood companies. By clarifying your goals and allocating the right resources, you could create targeted and cost-effective Facebook ads so as to power engagement, growth logo recognition, and ultimately raise your commercial enterprise's success inside the virtual realm.

Targeting Local Customers with Precision

In contemporary digital age, having a robust online presence is important for the success of any neighborhood commercial enterprise. And when it comes to on-line advertising and marketing, Facebook is undoubtedly one of the most powerful structures available. With its substantial consumer base and advanced concentrated on competencies, Facebook marketing has the potential to usher in a steady move of local clients like no different device.

This subchapter explores the art of targeting neighborhood clients with precision on Facebook, equipping local enterprise proprietors with the expertise and tools they want to maximise the capability of this platform. By implementing the strategies discussed here, you will be able to reach the right human beings at the proper time, ultimately boosting your sales and developing your purchaser base.

One of the key functions that makes Facebook marketing so effective for local groups is its advanced focused on alternatives. You can specify the location, age, gender, interests, or even conduct of your target market, making sure that your message reaches the ones most likely to be interested by your products or services. By narrowing down your focused on, you can avoid wasting your advertising finances on attaining folks that are unlikely to transform into clients.

Furthermore, Facebook's Local Awareness Ads permit you to goal customers to your on the spot place. This method that if you own a local coffee shop, as an example, you can target users who're currently within a selected radius of your location. This precise concentrated on lets in you to reach potential customers who are nearby and possibly to visit your established order.

Another powerful approach for targeting nearby clients on Facebook is leveraging the strength of person-generated content. Encourage your current clients to check-in, leave opinions, and share their stories to your web page. By doing so, you no longer most effective boom your visibility but also construct consider and credibility among capability clients who stumble upon your page.

In this subchapter, we are able to delve into the nitty-gritty of Facebook marketing for local businesses. From putting in place powerful targeting parameters to optimizing your advert content material, we will manual you via the technique little by little. By the cease, you will have a complete know-how of how to leverage Facebook's powerful equipment to attract and have interaction local customers, in the long run using your commercial enterprise towards achievement.

Creating Engaging Ad Creatives and Copy

In trendy digital age, Facebook advertising has grow to be an essential tool for local companies to attain their audience correctly. However, with millions of advertisements flooding customers' news feeds, it's crucial to create attractive advert creatives and charming replica that absolutely stand out. In this subchapter, we are able to explore the key strategies and strategies to help nearby groups master the art of making attractive advert creatives and replica on Facebook.

1. Know Your Audience: Understanding your audience is step one towards creating compelling advert creatives and replica. Conduct thorough studies to discover their hobbies, preferences, and ache points. This expertise will permit you to tailor your messaging to resonate with their desires and desires.

2. Visual Appeal: Visual content material is paramount on the subject of Facebook ads. Use amazing pix or motion pictures that are visually appealing and relevant in your enterprise. Ensure that your visuals are captivating and bring the essence of your emblem. Incorporate vibrant colors and compelling imagery to capture customers' attention amidst the cluttered information feeds.

3. Captivating Copy: The reproduction accompanying your ad have to be concise, impactful, and compelling. Craft a headline that grabs interest, conjures up curiosity, and entices customers to click on. Clearly

communicate the advantages of your products or services and highlight any specific promoting points that differentiate you from competitors. Use strength phrases, testimonials, and speak to-to-motion phrases to steer customers to take the favored movement.

four. A/B Testing: Experiment with different advert creatives and replica versions to determine which ones resonate most efficaciously along with your audience. Conduct A/B tests through walking more than one commercials concurrently, each with a mild variation in visuals or messaging. Analyze the overall performance metrics to discover the prevailing aggregate that drives the best engagement and conversions.

five. Personalization and Localization: Local groups have a unique benefit on Facebook as they are able to target specific geographical areas. Leverage this via personalizing your advert creatives and duplicate to mirror the local people. Incorporate neighborhood landmarks, activities, or language that resonates with your audience. This private contact will beautify the relationship between your enterprise and capability customers.

6. Compelling Call-to-Action: Every ad ought to have a clear call-to-action (CTA) that courses users in the direction of the favored action, consisting of creating a buy, signing up, or contacting your enterprise. Use motion-orientated verbs and create a sense of urgency to set off users to behave straight away.

By imposing these strategies for creating attractive advert creatives and copy on Facebook, local companies can significantly enhance their advertising efforts. Remember, the key is to recognize your audience, be visually attractive, craft compelling reproduction, behavior A/B checks, personalize for localization, and contain a compelling name-to-motion. With these techniques on your arsenal, you may be nicely to your way to studying Facebook advertising and reaching fulfillment in your neighborhood enterprise.

Chapter 13: Maximizing Face Book Marketing Tools

Utilizing Facebook Insights to Analyze Performance

One of the most effective equipment that neighborhood agencies can leverage for effective Facebook marketing is Facebook Insights. This function affords treasured data and analytics that can help local enterprise owners apprehend their target market, compare the fulfillment in their advertising efforts, and make knowledgeable decisions to optimize their Facebook method.

Understanding the demographics and behaviors of your target audience is essential for any local business. Facebook Insights provides comprehensive statistics in your web page's followers, together with their age, gender, vicinity, and language possibilities. Armed with this records, you can tailor your content material and advertising campaigns to better resonate with your target audience, resulting in increased engagement and conversions.

Another crucial component of Facebook Insights is publish-level data. This information permits neighborhood organizations to analyze the performance of person posts, assisting them perceive what kind of content resonates satisfactory with their target market. By assessing metrics including reach, engagement, and clicks, corporations can advantage insights into which posts are using the most site visitors, producing the maximum leads, or ensuing within the maximum conversions. Armed with this information, nearby agencies can mirror a hit posts and refine their content material strategy to maximize the effect of their Facebook advertising efforts.

Facebook Insights also gives treasured statistics on when your target audience is maximum energetic on the platform. By analyzing the facts on post reach and engagement over the years, local businesses can determine the most advantageous posting time table to ensure that their content material reaches as many ability customers as viable. This know-how can help companies keep away from posting at some point of periods of low pastime and recognition their efforts on instances while their audience is maximum likely to be on line, growing the chances of their posts being visible and engaged with.

Furthermore, Facebook Insights offers data on outside referrals, permitting local agencies to understand the sources that power visitors to their Facebook web page. By assessing which external web sites or social media platforms are sending the maximum visitors, corporations can perceive potential partnership opportunities and optimize their digital advertising techniques outdoor of Facebook.

In end, Facebook Insights is a powerful tool that nearby businesses can utilize to analyze the performance in their Facebook marketing efforts. By information their target market, comparing put up-stage facts, figuring out premiere posting instances, and studying external referrals, organizations could make statistics-driven selections to maximise the effectiveness in their Facebook marketing campaigns. By studying Facebook Insights, nearby corporations can advantage a competitive facet and reap extra fulfillment in their on-line advertising and marketing endeavors.

Harnessing the Power of Facebook Pixel for Local Business Success

In contemporary digital world, Facebook has become an important advertising device for local agencies. With its large user base and advanced targeting abilities, Facebook offers a completely unique opportunity for neighborhood organizations to reach and have interaction with their target market. One of the maximum powerful equipment in Facebook's arsenal is the Facebook Pixel.

The Facebook Pixel is a chunk of code that you may area to your website to accumulate facts and track person behavior. It lets in you to degree the effectiveness of your Facebook commercials, optimize your campaigns, and construct targeted audiences for destiny advertising and marketing efforts. By harnessing the energy of the Facebook Pixel, neighborhood companies can take their Facebook marketing strategy to the subsequent stage.

One of the important thing advantages of using the Facebook Pixel is its potential to tune conversions. Whether it is a purchase, a publication sign-up, or a contact shape submission, the Pixel can music those movements and provide treasured insights into the effectiveness of your advertisements. This records assist you to discover which commercials are driving the most conversions and make facts-driven decisions to optimize your campaigns.

Another benefit of the Facebook Pixel is its potential to create custom audiences. By monitoring person behavior to your website, you can build targeted audiences based on particular moves or pastimes. For example, if a person visits a product page however does not make a purchase, you could retarget them with a special bargain provide to encourage them to complete their purchase. This degree of personalization can substantially improve your conversion quotes and raise your common sales.

Furthermore, the Facebook Pixel can be used to optimize your commercials for specific goals. By leveraging the information collected by means of the Pixel, you could optimize your campaigns to attain individuals who are more likely to take a favored movement, such as making a buy or filling out a form. This guarantees that your advert budget is being spent on the maximum treasured and relevant audience, maximizing your return on investment.

For local agencies seeking to grasp Facebook advertising and marketing, harnessing the power of the Facebook Pixel is essential. By tracking conversions, developing custom audiences, and optimizing your advertisements, you may efficaciously reach and interact along with your target audience, ultimately driving greater visitors, leads, and sales on your business.

In conclusion, the Facebook Pixel is a game-changer for local corporations seeking to achieve Facebook advertising. By imposing and leveraging this powerful tool, you may gain treasured insights, optimize your campaigns, and achieve extraordinary success in reaching and engaging together with your target market. So, don't leave out out at the opportunity to harness the strength of the Facebook Pixel and take your neighborhood commercial enterprise to new heights in the virtual world.

Managing and Responding to Facebook Business Messages

As a neighborhood business proprietor, harnessing the electricity of Facebook advertising and marketing is crucial for achieving and tasty together with your audience. One of the most critical elements of this platform is coping with and responding to Facebook business messages effectively. In this subchapter, we will explore the strategies and techniques to help you master this crucial detail of Facebook advertising for local organizations.

The first step in handling Facebook enterprise messages is to make certain that you are actively tracking your inbox. Set apart devoted time each day to go through your messages and reply directly. Remember, well timed responses show your commitment to customer service and might assist construct believe and loyalty.

To streamline your message management process, don't forget using automation gear, which includes Facebook's Messenger Bot. These bots can cope with frequently requested questions, offer primary statistics, and even help in scheduling appointments or taking orders. However, it's miles critical to strike a balance among automation and personalization. While automation can store time, it's miles important to maintain a human contact and respond personally to unique queries and worries.

Crafting powerful responses is some other vital issue of managing Facebook business messages. Start with the aid of acknowledging the client's query or challenge after which provide a clean and concise answer or solution. Ensure that your tone is professional, pleasant, and reflective of your brand's voice. Remember, your responses are a mirrored image of your enterprise, and superb interactions can cause improved client delight and advocacy.

In addition to responding to messages, actively inspire clients to engage with your commercial enterprise via Facebook commercial enterprise messages. Promote the benefits of messaging, along with faster response times and personalized support. This will now not best decorate your customer support but additionally growth the chance of clients choosing your commercial enterprise over competition.

Furthermore, remember integrating Facebook Messenger into your customer support approach. By the usage of Messenger as a communication channel, you may offer real-time support, deal with purchaser inquiries successfully, or even provide personalized recommendations. This will now not simplest improve client pleasure however also help you build strong relationships with your target market.

In end, managing and responding to Facebook enterprise messages is a vital element of a success Facebook marketing for local groups. By actively tracking your inbox, utilizing automation gear appropriately, crafting powerful responses, and inspiring engagement, you can decorate your customer service, build agree with, and in the long run force business increase.

Exploring Facebook Live for Local Business Promotions

In modern digital age, social media structures have become powerful gear for nearby agencies to connect to their target audience and promote their products or services effectively. Among these platforms, Facebook holds a dominant position, offering numerous functions for corporations to engage with their customers. One such characteristic that stands out is Facebook Live, a live streaming service that permits businesses to broadcast their content in real-time to their fans.

Facebook Live gives nearby corporations a completely unique opportunity to exhibit their logo, have interaction with their target market, and raise their on line presence. By harnessing the electricity of live video, businesses can create a greater authentic and private reference to their customers, leading to improved agree with and brand loyalty.

One of the key blessings of using Facebook Live for local enterprise promotions is its potential to reach a huge target market immediately. With a unmarried click, companies can go live and percentage exciting news, product launches, in the back of-the-scenes pictures, or maybe host Q&A sessions. This actual-time interaction lets in corporations to cope with purchaser queries, offer instantaneous feedback, and construct a experience of community around their emblem.

Moreover, Facebook Live gives precious analytics that may assist agencies measure the achievement of their live videos. By tracking metrics including the variety of viewers, engagement prices, and viewer remarks, businesses can advantage insights into their target audience's choices and tailor their destiny content for that reason.

Another compelling element of Facebook Live is its ability to generate buzz and appeal to interest. By promoting upcoming live streams earlier, groups can create anticipation among their fans and encourage them to music in. This can be accomplished thru attractive posts, e mail newsletters, or collaborations with influencers of their area of interest. By leveraging the power of Facebook Live, local groups can growth their on-line visibility and attain a much wider target market.

In end, Facebook Live is a powerful device for nearby corporations seeking to enhance their Facebook advertising and marketing techniques. By utilizing this option, companies can have interaction with their target market in real-time, construct consider, and create a experience of community. Additionally, the analytics furnished by Facebook Live can help corporations refine their content and reach their audience greater correctly. By embracing this innovative tool, neighborhood corporations can take their Facebook advertising and marketing to the next level and acquire their promotional desires.

Chapter 14: Effective Strategies

Implementing Effective Content Marketing Tactics

In modern-day virtual panorama, content material fabric fabric marketing has come to be an imperative method for neighborhood businesses to thrive on Facebook. By growing and meting out treasured, applicable, and everyday content material fabric fabric, groups can entice and engage their goal market, ultimately riding extra traffic, leads, and conversions. This subchapter will discover the important strategies that community groups can put in force to understand content material fabric advertising and advertising and marketing on Facebook.

1. Understanding Your Target Audience: The first step in powerful content material fabric advertising and marketing and advertising and marketing is to find out and understand your target marketplace. Local companies should conduct thorough marketplace research to advantage insights into their customers'

demographics, pursuits, and ache elements. This information will manual the creation of content material that resonates with their goal market.

2. Creating Engaging Content: Local businesses should recognition on developing brilliant content fabric this is informative, thrilling, and shareable. This can include weblog posts, movies, infographics, and patron testimonials. By supplying cost to their audience, agencies can installation themselves as company experts and construct trust with their clients.

3. Utilizing Multimedia: To captivate Facebook users' interest, neighborhood companies ought to include severa sorts of multimedia content material fabric. Incorporate stunning pix, movement pictures, and interactive content into your posts to motive them to greater visually attractive and appealing. This will boom the opportunity of your content material cloth material being shared and accomplishing a far broader target market.

4. Consistency and Frequency: To keep your target marketplace engaged, it is vital to maintain a constant content material material time table. Businesses need to create a chunk of writing calendar and make sure normal postings. However, it's miles similarly vital to strike a stability and keep away from overwhelming your goal marketplace with excessive content material material, which may additionally furthermore cause unfollows or unlikes.

5. Leveraging User-Generated Content: Encouraging clients to percent their studies and tales associated with your enterprise can be a powerful content fabric advertising and advertising and marketing tactic. User-generated content material cloth not most effective affords authenticity however moreover will increase engagement and fosters a feel of network. Local corporations can incentivize clients to make a contribution by means of way of using strolling contests or offering their content material cloth material on their Facebook web web page.

6. Tracking and Analyzing Performance: To diploma the achievement of your content material cloth fabric advertising efforts, nearby corporations need to frequently check key metrics including reach, engagement, and conversions. Facebook Insights gives precious data that might assist optimize your content method and make knowledgeable choices for future campaigns.

In conclusion, enforcing powerful content fabric advertising and marketing strategies is vital for network agencies to maximize their presence on Facebook. By records their goal marketplace, creating appealing content material cloth, making use of multimedia, keeping consistency, leveraging character-generated content material cloth, and tracking ordinary overall performance, organizations can create a strong on-line presence, enhance logo consciousness, and power tangible results.

Partnering with Local Influencers and Collaborations

In ultra-contemporary digital age, Facebook advertising and advertising and marketing has turn out to be an crucial tool for network organizations to connect with their target market successfully. One approach that could considerably improve your on-line presence and engagement on Facebook is partnering with close by influencers and collaborations.

Local influencers are people who've a terrific following on social media systems, specifically Facebook, and very very own have an impact on over their audience's shopping for alternatives. Collaborating with those influencers will allow you to obtain a much wider goal market and benefit credibility inside your network.

First and important, perceive influencers who align at the side of your brand values and goal marketplace. Look for influencers with a first-rate neighborhood following and engagement fees. These influencers want to have an actual voice and a actual hobby to your corporation. Reach out to them with a customized message, highlighting why you consider a partnership may be useful for every sports.

When partnering with network influencers, it's essential to establish easy goals and expectations. Clearly outline what you choice to advantage thru the collaboration, whether or not it is advanced emblem recognition, higher engagement, or using profits. Discuss how the partnership may be collectively beneficial, and make certain that every activities are on the same page concerning deliverables, timelines, and reimbursement if applicable.

Collaborations with community influencers can take numerous workplace paintings. They can create sponsored content fabric offering your services or products, take part in activities or giveaways, or provide testimonials and critiques. By leveraging their have an impact on and credibility, you could tap into their goal marketplace and generate hobby on your commercial enterprise company.

Another effective approach for Facebook advertising and advertising and marketing for close by companies is taking thing with distinctive neighborhood companies. Seek out non-competitive corporations that percentage a comparable target market. Join forces to create joint advertising and marketing campaigns, skip-sell every one of a kind's offerings, or maybe host joint sports or workshops. Such collaborations now not best make bigger your achieve however moreover beautify your credibility within the network. By pooling assets and leveraging every unique's strengths, you can create a win-win scenario for all involved.